MEDIA RELATIONS FOR SCHOOLS

Including Crisis Communications

CHERI LOVRE

Solution Tree

Cover art and design by Grannan Graphic Design Ltd.
Printed in the United States of America
ISBN 1-932127-89-5

IF YOUR SCHOOL IS IN CRISIS, TURN TO PAGE 93

If you are using this resource for planning and organization, turn to the table of contents (page vii).

Other Resources by Cheri Lovre

Administrator's Grab and Go Briefcase

All Staff Preparedness Training Package

Catastrophic Events Resource Manual

Crisis Resource Manual

Emergency Kit CD

Grab and Go Duffel

Reclaiming Life! A Workbook for Survivors of Trauma

The Day That . . . A Workbook for Youth in the Aftermath of Trauma

The Safe Room: A Guide for School Crisis Responders

Visit the Crisis Management Institute (CMI) web site at www.cmionline.org for other materials and more information about crisis training. As a service to schools, CMI posts guidelines for administrators, counselors, teachers, and parents in the aftermath of major events. These are free to download and distribute, as long as the copyright information is left intact at the bottom of every page.

Acknowledgments

The author would like to thank the following people for their capable assistance in bringing this resource together. A huge thanks to Rosemary Pryor, communications/intergovernmental relations director, City of Springfield, Oregon, for her sage advice and keen editing eye. Thanks also to Ron Steiner of the Marketing Communications Group; Cherie Kistner, public information officer, Springfield School District, Oregon; and Shannon Priem, Oregon School Boards Association, for their helpful comments. Tim Buckley of Buckley Communications organized the materials and helped with writing and editing of an early version of the final product.

Table of Contents

About the Author

Cheri Lovre, M.S., is a nationally recognized expert in school crisis and trauma response and prevention with more than 30 years of experience assisting schools in the aftermath of tragedy.

She provides crisis response training and technical assistance to schools as well as a variety of emergency services agencies, victim advocacy groups, trauma responders, and employee assistance providers. Her clients include the National Association of Secondary School Principals, the American Association of School Administrators, the National Rural Education Association, and the Association of Educational Service Agencies.

Ms. Lovre is the founder and director of the Crisis Management Institute in Salem, Oregon.

Introduction

On a Friday evening in a small blue-collar town nestled in the mountains, a house fire resulted in the tragic deaths of three school children. Television satellite trucks from several stations in fairly distant metropolitan areas converged on the tiny community. Over the weekend, the story became featured news throughout the state.

This community was part of a collaborative county-wide crisis response system, so by Monday morning, a good number of trained, experienced adults had arrived to provide support to grieving students across all grades. The day was going as well as possible in light of the circumstances. Each of the three empty desks had beautiful bouquets on them, and students were leaving cards and letters they had created for the families on those desks.

And then, outside the window of a second-story classroom, the satellite dish from one of the media trucks rose into view. As soon as the students saw it, they dashed to the windows, opened them, and yelled down to the reporters, "Leave us alone!" and, "Go home!" The mood shifted abruptly from sadness and grief to anger and distraction. An otherwise calm and meaningful time became a circus.

This event shows how pervasive and persistent the media can be in a crisis, even in a remote community. Because the media's presence and influence can be so intense, a school's best strategy is to proactively develop positive media relations ahead of time. Throughout a normal school year, many other less urgent situations arise that still demand a response from school administrators. The media has incredible potential to influence public perception of the school—for better or for worse.

News coverage during calmer times can highlight your school's achievements, create a sense of excitement about education, and stimulate increased parent and community involvement in school activities and programs. If you are only responding to bad press coverage, you are missing an opportunity to build positive relationships when you have the time and energy, before the crisis arises.

Media relations depend on one pivotal concept: relationship. Nothing will provide a school or district with more leverage in the community than having a good, established relationship with the press, particularly in a crisis situation. When that positive relationship exists, "managing the media" becomes "media relations." This is the best of all possible worlds, and in a crisis, it is absolutely essential.

Effective media relations includes understanding the media and its tools, planning for general and crisis media relations, and using the media to promote the school's message. This resource will help you develop your own priorities and guide your thinking on working with media. "You" may be a team serving a district or just one person serving one school; you may work on media relations full-time, or you may have to juggle it with another position; your title may be media liaison, principal, public relations director, or even head librarian. For simplicity, this resource will refer to the person in charge of media relations as the *public information officer,* or *PIO.* Because districts differ greatly in size, no single approach or set of guidelines will work uniformly. Media strategies must be tailored to your particular situation. The worst mistake is to have no strategy at all.

Please note that this resource focuses on general media relations for schools, with specific guidance for media relations during school-related crises. *Media relations is only one piece of crisis response; crisis management involves many other urgent aspects.* For more information on planning and response to crisis, grief, and trauma, please consult the *Crisis Resource Manual,* the *Catastrophic Events Resource Manual,* and *The Safe Room* by Cheri Lovre, available from Crisis Management Institute and Solution Tree.

Chapter 1

Understanding the Media

• • • • • • • • • • • • • • • • • • • •

Media Needs

To make media relations work to your advantage, you must first understand the media's needs and priorities. The media's first concern is to get the story and to get it on time. Reporters are competing for the best story—the most complete, accurate, and interesting story possible—and they must meet rigid deadlines. The more impact an event has, the greater the presence and potential influence of the media. Competition is fierce, and when the potential for significant news exists, integrity and sensitivity may take a back seat to winning the war for the best story.

During the regular school year, you may have to work to convince reporters and editors that a positive story about a new after-school program, a particularly talented teacher, or a recent grant for infrastructure improvements serves their need for news and not just the school's need for publicity. More importantly, any news coverage you do secure should communicate the *school's* message, rather than allow the media to find its own (possibly negative) interpretation. Understanding how to frame the school's message in terms of the media's needs is critical to successful media relations.

In a crisis, however, reporters may go well beyond your comfort zone to gather information. A crisis presents opportunities for many stories, and the public will clamor for details—and rightfully so. The better prepared you are to supply the media with the timely, pertinent, and reliable information they need, the greater the chances that the media will respect school policy and the boundaries you have established to protect your school and its staff, students, and families.

Media Roles

The media can be a powerful ally in a school's efforts to communicate with a large audience. Unlike a newsletter or notices sent home with students, a feature in a newspaper or on television or radio reaches those who do not yet have a connection with your school, but may in the future. This includes potential students, parents, staff, and school board members; members of the business community not currently involved in partnerships with your school; taxpayers who may vote on bond issues; local and government officials who may have input into funding and legislation; and many others. Positive media coverage establishes credibility, builds awareness, and facilitates networking with your current and potential stakeholders.

Having already created strong relationships with the media will serve your school well when community debate erupts over controversial curriculums, disappointing standardized test scores, or other occasions for official explanations or apologies. If the media finds your school's response insufficient, uncooperative, or combative, they will not hesitate to spread that news as well. As the old saying in journalism warns, "Don't do battle with someone who buys ink by the barrel," especially when the news is bad. With the media on your side, your chances of emerging unscathed—or even stronger—are greatly improved.

In a true crisis, media coverage is a crucial element of crisis management. Good coverage is key to overcoming rumor and public panic, as well as to establishing confidence that the school is handling the crisis skillfully and appropriately. Timely news coverage minimizes the gathering of onlookers and reduces the spread of rumor. Television and radio can disseminate critical information—which roads are closed for emergency services, where parents can pick up children, and what phone numbers to call and Internet sites to visit for more information—very effectively. The media can also educate the public by sharing life-saving information, such as the warning signs of depression, for example, after the death of a local teenager by suicide. A media invested in a partnering relationship with the school and its crisis response team can help a community more quickly turn the corner from crisis to recovery.

Media Dynamics

The presence of the media changes everything. In a crisis that attracts national attention, media presence can create profound logistical and communication problems. Satellite dish

Breaking the Cycle

In a rapidly growing rural community, four students died by what appeared to be suicide within 3 weeks of each other (one death may have been an accidental overdose.) Everyone was overwhelmed—teachers, parents, students, and administrators.

Initially, the media interviewed parents who were critical of the school, who had inflammatory messages, and who made the story more controversial. Then school media officials called a news conference to point out that the media's portrayal of the suicides could either cost student lives, by glamorizing suicide, or save student lives, by educating students and their parents.

Afterwards, the media's treatment of the event shifted. The press began giving information on how to talk with children about suicide, how to watch for signs of depression, and how to contact local mental health resources. Over the following weeks, reporters continued to take stories and suggestions from school counselors, administrators, and others to help the community understand that responsibility for preventing suicide rests with everyone, not just our schools.

trucks aggravate traffic issues, clutter the memorial zones that spontaneously emerge, and impose lights, noise, and a circus-like atmosphere at a time when private reflection and silent social gatherings would be more helpful. Those in positions of authority and responsibility find their most important duties complicated or blocked. Additionally, media presence disturbs the atmosphere, increases the level of drama, and distracts grievers from coping. Major networks offer thousands of dollars to families who have been in the eye of the storm, and it is often difficult for families to refuse to speak with a famous anchor person from a major television network. Chapter 4 will explore how schools can control media dynamics in a crisis to protect their staff, students, and families from this kind of exploitation.

One of the unfortunate side effects of the electronic age is that some standards of common sense and human decency become less valued: As the journalism adage notes, "If it bleeds, it leads." In the aftermath of Princess Diana's death, for example, great controversy erupted over whether to show pictures of her dying in the back of the crumpled car. The media ultimately decided that these pictures were not respectful of her, her family, or the viewing audience. And yet on one network television newscast, the story *following* Princess Di's death focused on the gory details of a man who had entered a building armed with weapons and emerged later to shoot himself in the parking lot.

Although the media had decided it was not dignified to show Princess Di's death scene, in the case of this ordinary person, no special consideration was given: Television helicopters hovered over his dead body while the voice of the reporter gave the sordid details. In other cases, the media has played the tapes of 911 calls made by those who have just found the body of a child, with little or no concern for the reaction of families whose most private moment of grief has been exposed to the world. New technology has made accessing such pivotal moments easier than ever: Students with cell phones can capture and e-mail images of death scenes before school or local authorities know that anything has occurred.

Intrusion is part of the price a culture must pay for the instant and intimate news coverage it has come to expect and demand. There are times when the media can actually cause unnecessary additional trauma to victims, their families, and the community. In conversations with principals whose schools have experienced a catastrophic event, no single issue is more frequently raised than the challenge of handling media effectively in the midst of crisis.

Emotions on Stage

In the aftermath of a school shooting covered by national media, reporters aggressively approached youth who had gathered at the memorial wall to leave flowers, teddy bears, and cards (a memorial wall is often spontaneously created in the aftermath of these events). Some reporters offered students money to cry on camera. Some asked students to talk about the victims or the alleged perpetrators. Others filmed the religious groups that appeared at the memorial wall to pray, speak in tongues, or solicit converts, thus encouraging an already confusing and dramatic encounter between grieving students and forceful strangers.

The camera has a very seductive quality, but appearing on television can have detrimental effects for the individual as well as the school. In this age of sound bites, most "person on the street" interviews are reduced to sentences and phrases that, when aired, may be taken out of context. Staff and students who see themselves on camera may experience a letdown when their intended message is not conveyed. If they were still suffering from shock or feeling traumatized at the time of the interview, their comments may appear to lack feeling or may convey a transitory sentiment that becomes embarrassing only hours later.

Unfortunately, those who rush forward at the opportunity to speak into a camera after a crisis will often be those least suited to represent the school: adults or children with a grudge or a peculiar interpretation of events. They may reveal information the police need to keep confidential for their ongoing investigation, or they may unwittingly direct media attention to other individuals or families. Publicity also exposes children to dangers beyond regret or embarrassment. In several cases of publicized school crises, youth who spoke with reporters and whose names were flashed across the bottom of the television screen had to deal later with stalkers who looked up their families' home phone numbers. This introduced a new frightening element to the crisis.

Comments made by media interviewers in the aftermath of the Littleton, Colorado, shooting on April 21, 1999, indicated their belief that "grief therapy by media" was helpful for students, but over time it became evident that those students who were "media stars" had put off their grieving. When the media moved on to new stories, students released from stardom found themselves far behind their peers in processing the loss. Children need time to process tragedy and then integrate its meaning into their lives. It is rarely helpful for them to endure immediate probing and scrutiny by the press.

Reporters will sometimes resort to deceitful tactics to elicit information and interviews with children and adults. To gain access to off-limits areas, they may crawl through windows or disguise themselves as a concerned parent or even as a school staff member. They may don medical disguises to get into hospital rooms or pose as insurance claim adjusters to gain access to victims' private lives. After one school shooting, a reporter went to the home of the vice principal of the high school. She posed as a concerned community member who was helping identify the dead and wounded and told the vice principal's wife that he had sent her to get last year's annual to confirm their identifications. Who could say no to that? Some of the first publicized photographs of the victims and the perpetrator of that particular shooting were never released by families, but rather were the result of this deceit.

Local media representatives may be more helpful than national network or cable reporters, because they have to continue living in the community. They may already have some connection to the school, either through having attended the school or knowing families whose children attend the school. They may have reported on school sports or other school-related business and thus may already be familiar with school staff and media policies. In one community, for example, when a beloved teacher and coach died by suicide on school grounds during the school day, the media tempered their coverage with compassion because the deceased was so well-known and liked by reporters for promoting positive athletic opportunities for all students. Be careful not to play favorites with local media, however; any hint of one reporter getting a special "scoop" encourages others to take drastic measures to find a better scoop.

The good news is that individual journalists are like city managers, social workers, school teachers, police officers, paramedics, and elected officials: They believe they are working for a higher purpose on behalf of the public good. At their best, journalists facilitate the resolution of crisis through factual reporting. And as individuals, they are just as vulnerable to post–traumatic stress disorder as a result of being on the scene or viewing traumatic footage as any of your school staff. But the news industry is not sensitive to the psychology of trauma. The media accommodates neither the well-being of your staff and students nor the long-term mental health of its own reporters.

Tips for Handling Public or Press Criticism

- Do your research and be factual.

- Invite input from the public.

- Record everything.

- Do not promise to solve the problem.

- Always start with a positive.

- Make personal contact.

- If complaints are justified, admit it, and explain the reasons behind the problem.

- Sympathize and empathize.

- Always be friendly.

- Respond quickly.

- Do not use jargon.

(Adapted from Woodland, 2003)

Successful media relations uses media tools and planning to manage the effects of the media on all parties—to ensure that the media gets the story without undue harm or risk to children, adults, or such intangibles as reputation and image. The tone set by media coverage influences the public's interpretation of events. If a teacher is convicted on criminal charges, for example, the media's "take" might suggest that the school does not adequately screen personnel and that parents should be concerned about the safety of their children. Alternatively, the same story might focus on the students' sadness and the school's use of the event as a teachable moment to talk about character and the law.

Effective media relations can also encourage positive parent and community involvement in the school. During the regular school year, the media's coverage of an event—a board meeting to review budget priorities, a public meeting for parents and administration to discuss redistricting, a Friday-night football game or a regional quiz-bowl match—establishes the event's significance and indirectly (or directly) encourages the public to get involved. This resource will help you take an active role in controlling media dynamics so that the *right* stories appear.

This candid discussion is not meant to disparage journalism or its purpose. However, school administrators are always surprised by the powerful presence of the media. The onslaught of media attention can be incredible, and its effect is almost always underestimated. In a small town, a single article can create a bad impression that lingers for years. After an event like a school shooting, hundreds of media personnel may come to town, and it only takes a handful of reporters who resort to unacceptable means to change the climate of the community and to overwhelm school administrators, staff, students, and families. Learning to use the media's tools to your own advantage and planning for media relations will create a better outcome for your school *and* better stories for the media. The next section will outline those tools.

Chapter 2

Media Tools

Chapter Overview

Sections

Samples and Checklists

(continued)

Chapter Overview (continued)

Samples and Checklists (continued)

- Sample Crisis Media Advisory (page 43)
- Media Advisory Checklist (page 44)
- Sample News Conference Agenda (page 50)
- News Conference Checklist (page 55)
- Sample School History (page 58)
- Sample School Fact Sheet (page 60)
- Press Kit Checklist (page 62)

• • • • • • • • • • • • • • • • • • • •

Media relations is a tool for *public* relations: Organizations and individuals establish relationships with the media to further their relationships with the public. Even though your end goal is to send a certain message to the public, you must keep in mind that the media is the intermediary. The media decides whether it will relay your message, and the media filters the content of any message it does publish or broadcast. As the school or district's media liaison or public information officer (PIO), your goal should be to increase the number of messages that the media relays and to ensure that the media filters those messages as little as possible. To that purpose, you can learn to use the media's own tools to your advantage.

Media relations works best when all parties in the school or district administration understand the chain of command for developing and approving press materials. All parties must also be aware of the time-sensitive nature of media relations and be committed to supplying information and approving drafts in a timely fashion. Be sure that the school or district has policies in place (for more information, see page 64) that define what may (and may not) be covered and who gives final approval to drafts. If your district has special public image problems, you may want to work with the administration to pinpoint specific goals and the kinds of news stories that would achieve those goals. In addition, you will need to assemble and maintain a media directory of current media contacts to ensure that your approved media relations documents reach the right people (for more information on planning for effective media relations, see chapter 3, beginning on page 63).

Building positive media relations takes time and care, but it is possible. The media needs news, and stories about children and education are important to media stakeholders. Even achieving a modest goal of one story a month in the local paper will help your school's public image, and each media contact you establish makes the next story that much easier to secure. Community newspapers and television stations will sometimes create a regular section or segment for school coverage, possibly even coproduced with students.

Practice using media tools when the news is good. You may think you are too busy, but in a crisis, you will truly be too busy—and too late—to build positive relations when you most need it. This chapter will address the five main tools of media relations: public service announcements, press releases, media advisories, press conferences, and press kits.

Public Service Announcements

Public service announcements, or PSAs, are the most direct way to reach the public through radio or television, since broadcasters read exactly what you submit to them. Guidelines for submission and formatting vary, so always contact your local stations or check their web sites first. Remember that public stations may be more accessible than commercial stations, and take advantage of their commitment to serving the community.

Placement of a PSA requires a personal media contact. Send your PSA to the attention of someone you know, and be sure that person is expecting to receive it. There are very few opportunities for television public service announcements, and stations receive many requests. They often require all PSAs to be preproduced. Request a television PSA only for major projects or occasions.

A radio PSA is easier to produce, especially if the station requires you to record your own PSA. Radio PSAs are short (usually 15–30 seconds long) and contain one message meant to convey information useful to the public. Many stations only accept PSAs from tax-exempt organizations. A PSA might include the location and times for a meeting of an adult literacy program, for example, or might remind students not to drink and drive on prom night. A PSA runs for a limited period of time specified by the submitting organization. Usually, the rules for content and length are strict. Superlatives like "best," "greatest," and so on are forbidden, for example, as are calls to action like "Sign up today!" However, PSAs may instruct listeners to call for more information.

An announcer reads a PSA exactly as it is written; formats vary, but usually a PSA is written in the third person. An announcement for radio can be more spontaneous or playful in tone, but an announcement for television should sound like news. Public service announcements should be printed on letterhead and double-spaced (use all capital letters for a radio PSA). The upper left corner should show your contact name and title, plus phone numbers for day and evening contact. The upper right corner gives the date range in which the station should air the PSA. Center the title (and for radio, the time length of the PSA) mid-page, before the text. Put "- end -" at the end of the PSA (Miller, 2005).

A PSA should be easy for the announcer to read, so try reading it aloud yourself before sending it in. For television announcements that are not preproduced, you may be allowed to send digital images to accompany the message. But many stations will *insist* that you preproduce your own PSA; check their guidelines. You may be able to involve your school's audiovisual staff and students in the production of the announcement.

A public service announcement is a small way to remind the community that your school or district provides valuable services and cares about its staff, students, and their families. A radio PSA is free, direct, and a good way to ease yourself into media relations.

Crisis PSAs

A public service announcement is not appropriate for use in a crisis, because it requires too much advance notice to integrate into a radio or television station's programming. After a crisis, however, you may find PSAs helpful to broadcast general information. After a teen suicide, for example, you might submit an announcement that lists the signs of depression and provides national or local hotline numbers for help. After other crises, your PSA might focus on the meeting times of support groups, safety reminders, or other relevant information.

Sample Radio PSA

```
                    [letterhead]

Contact: Mamie Jones, Public Information Officer
Phone: (310) 555-5555 ext. 555
Night line: (310) 555-5555

Begin Oct. 1
End Oct. 15

        30-SECOND PSA — WINTER COAT DRIVE

COLD WEATHER IS HERE, AND GUESS WHAT? JOE JUNIOR

FINALLY HIT THAT GROWTH SPURT AND CAN'T WEAR HIS

OLD COAT ANYMORE. JANE JUNIOR SAVED HER MONEY

AND BOUGHT A NEW COAT SHE LIKES BETTER THAN THE

ONE GRANDMA GAVE HER.

GOOD NEWS, MOM! LINCOLN HIGH IS HAVING ITS

ANNUAL DRIVE FOR CLEAN, GENTLY USED WINTER

COATS. CLEAN OUT YOUR CLOSET AND KEEP SOMEONE

TOASTY WARM THIS WINTER. COATS FOR ALL AGES AND

SIZES WILL BE COLLECTED AT FRIDAY NIGHT'S

BASKETBALL GAME AND AT LINCOLN HIGH AUDITORIUM

UNTIL OCTOBER 16TH. CALL 555-1212 FOR MORE

INFORMATION.

                    - end -
```

Media Relations for Schools • Copyright © 2007 by Cheri Lovre
Solution Tree • www.solution-tree.com

Sample Broadcast PSA

[letterhead]

Contact: Mamie Jones, Public Information Officer
Phone: (310) 555-5555 ext. 555
Night line: (310) 555-5555

Begin Oct. 1
End Oct. 15

ANNUAL WINTER COAT DRIVE AT LINCOLN HIGH

Lincoln High's annual winter coat drive will kick off on October 4 at Friday night's basketball game against Jefferson High. Clean coats in good condition will be collected and distributed to needy families throughout the county.

This is the fourth year for the coat drive, which is organized by the Lincoln High student council in association with county trustees.

Last year, Lincoln High collected 300 coats. This year's goal is 400.

Coats will be collected at Friday night's game and at Lincoln High Auditorium until October 16. All sizes and styles of clean, gently used coats for adults and children are welcome.

Call 555-1212 for more information.

- end -

Public Service Announcement Checklist

•••••••••••••••••••••

____ Study the station's PSA guidelines.

____ Meet the submission guidelines for content, and follow the suggested technical format exactly.

____ Write an easy-to-read-aloud announcement that takes as long as it says at the top to read: no more, no less.

____ Do not include calls to action, superlatives, or other forbidden elements.

____ Give the station ample advance notice, according to its suggested guidelines, and indicate the time frame to run the announcement.

____ Deliver the announcement to the correct person, in the form preferred by that person (e-mail or fax).

____ Indicate your contact information in case the station has questions.

Press Releases

A press release is a one- or two- page document that includes a statement of information or a story prepared for the news media. It should inform the media of a good story, influence the media's perception and portrayal of an ongoing story, or prompt the media to conduct an interview. An effective press release convinces the media not just to run a story, but to run it in a way that favors the school.

There are many obvious occasions to send a press release—for example, if your school has just won a state, provincial, or national award for school improvement or high test scores—but there are many smaller occasions that can be presented in a way that makes them newsworthy. *A press release is your means to control when and how news about your school appears.* Using a press release, instead of just calling and requesting an interview, gives you time to formulate exactly what you would like the article to say: A written statement reduces the risk of misquotes and misinterpretations. A press release is also faster and easier for the reporter than setting up an interview, thinking of questions, coordinating with a photographer, and so on. If a positive story about your school or district has not appeared in your local press recently, a press release will help you build relationships with media representatives and remind your stakeholders of the excellence of your school.

Always be sure that your press release has been approved by the appropriate school or district authority before sending it out. Work with your school board and administrative staff to establish a chain of command that can review and approve press releases in a timely fashion. Make sure that anyone quoted in your press release has the opportunity to review the quote in its context, before the press release is sent out.

How to "Make" News

- Issue a report.

- Arrange or give a speech to the community, parents, students, or staff.

- Celebrate an anniversary.

- Announce plans to build, purchase new materials, or hire special staff.

- Form and announce names for committees and appointments.

- Present an award or commendation to a teacher, staff member, or student.

- Pass a resolution.

- Stage a special event with ties to current events or your community.

- Organize a tour or open house.

- Help students promote their reports, student council resolutions, and special projects.

(Adapted from Wilcox, Ault, and Agee, 1992, as cited in Hallahan, 1996)

A press release is always written in the third person, in a journalistic style, as if it were an actual article appearing in the paper. In fact, the closer the printed article is to your press release, the better—that way you control the content. A press release begins with a headline that catches the editor's attention.

Its first or "lead" paragraph gets right to the point with the most important information and gives the 5 Ws of journalism: who, what, where, when, and why—how is also included.

When considering your headline and your lead, ask yourself, "*Who* is doing *what* that is important, and *how* can I say that in one sentence?" Similarly, ask yourself how you can phrase "when and where" to mean "here and now" (Miller, 2005). For example, in a story about a debate team traveling to a state competition in 6 weeks, your headline could say, "Local students win right to compete at state" to emphasize what the students have already accomplished at home, rather than what might happen in 6 weeks somewhere else.

Do not "bury the lead" by introducing important characters or facts late in your press release. Everything critical should appear in your first paragraph. Later paragraphs should be no longer than three sentences each. Highlight details and facts that address the features of a good story *as media understand them.*

A press release uses quotes throughout, just like a real news story. To make it easier on all parties, when you ask administrators or others featured in your press release for a quote, give them sample sentences that show what kind of statement is helpful. They may just "sign off" on your sample. If they respond with long original quotes, select only those parts that serve your press release. Quotes should provide fresh information to keep the story moving forward.

Like a real story, a press release should not contain obviously self-promoting language or "marketing-ese." Remember, it should sound as though it were written by a reporter, not a

What Makes a Good Story?

Relevance: Will the subject have a powerful impact in this community now or in the near future?

Topicality: Does the subject tie in with other current events and hot issues?

Human interest: Does the story contain interesting characters or evoke an emotional response?

Visual interest: Could the story be accompanied by compelling visuals?

Narrative interest:

- Is the story or its subject controversial?

- Does the story contain conflict followed by resolution?

- Does the story present a fresh take on a familiar subject?

- Does the story have practical value ("how to" or "self-help" information)?

(Adapted from Schiller, 2004, and Ryan, 1991, as cited in Hallahan, 1996)

school representative or a salesperson. Do not write or use a quote saying, for example, that a new after-school reading program is "the best in the country" or that "John Doe School really cares and proudly announces a wonderful reading program." Instead, write, "The school has opened two extra sessions to accommodate the demand for the program," or quote an administrator saying, "We saw that this program improved test scores for children at City Elementary by 50%, and we wanted to give our kids that chance."

A press release serves three parties: the school, the media, and the public. The sometimes unspoken *message* of the press release—"Our school is proactive about reading"—matters to the school. The *news angle*—"Literacy is a hot topic in our area right now; the photo of the kid giving the thumbs up to the teacher is great"—matters to the editor. The *facts and organization*—"Where can I sign up my child? Is this program just a fad?"—matter to the reader (Miller, 2005).

Keep a press release short and sweet; it should never be longer than 500 words (two double-spaced pages). One page is the best length, and it must be double-spaced. A press release always has contact information in case a reporter wants to know more.

A press release follows very specific formatting rules. In a crisis, the media probably will not care if you follow these rules. But knowing the rules and following them establishes your professionalism and credibility. For metropolitan schools or districts, professionalism is essential to getting that edge with busy editors. For small-town schools, being comfortable with the rules may come in handy in a crisis that attracts national media; you will need all the leverage and authority you can get to stand up to their aggressive tactics and pressure.

The bottom line is, if you have the time to write a press release, take the time to do it right. There are plenty of advantages to following the rules. Do not let the formatting guidelines discourage you. Once you have a created a template file, you can add new content quickly.

Press Release Formatting 101

- Send the press release on letterhead.

- At the top left, below the letterhead, put the contact's name and title, e-mail address, phone number, and a "night line": a number a reporter working late can call to get last-minute details.

- At the top right, put the date and either the words "FOR IMMEDIATE RELEASE" in all capitals or "FOR RELEASE ON _____ [date]."

- Leave some space before the headline, in case the editor wants to write a comment there.

- Center the headline and use all capital letters. Create a headline that instantly conveys the story and its subject.

- Use 1-inch margins and a 12-point font. Double-space so that the reporter can edit his or her piece using your actual press release.

- Include a "dateline"—city, state, and date of the story—before your first sentence.

- Keep it to one page whenever possible, and never longer than two pages. Make sure the first page breaks at the end of a paragraph.

- If you have two pages, the first page should say "- more -" at the bottom, and the second page should say "PAGE TWO" in the upper right corner. The upper left corner should contain a "slug line," a shortened version of your headline. The second page should say "- last -" at the bottom.

- Do not write over two pages!

(Adapted from Miller, 2005)

Media Tools

Maintain a *media directory* that identifies reporters, their organizations, contact information, and preferred form of communication (by e-mail or by fax). If you do not know these things, call and ask. Keep a record with each press release of who received it, who responded (and when and how), and whether a story appeared as a result. Compare all stories to your initial press release, and archive a copy with your records. Finally, correct any errors that appear in the story.

Correcting News Errors

1. Make the correction in writing. A phone call puts everyone on the spot.

2. Pick your battles. A minor error in a generally supportive article is just that—minor. If you correct it, be sure to include the correction as one small part of a thank-you letter that focuses on the article's strengths and its importance to your school.

3. Stay calm and focus on the facts. A major error or omission must be corrected; send a copy of your letter to both the editor and the reporter. Point out the mistake objectively, and support your position with facts. Show appreciation for positive coverage, and offer to further clarify if necessary.

4. Don't criticize the reporter or the media organization to the public. If outraged parents, teachers, or administrators point out the error to you, simply say you are working with the paper or station to correct it. Future coverage of your school will benefit from your discretion and tact.

(Adapted from Schindler, 2004)

If you send your press release by e-mail, create a meaningful subject line that makes it clear your e-mail is not spam. Do not use all capital letters, exclamation points, dollar signs, or other forms of emphasis in your subject line. Make your subject line specific: "Lincoln Students Learn New Way to Read" is better than "Press Release From School," for example. Attach the press release to the e-mail so that the document's original formatting is retained; sometimes press releases that have been cut and pasted into the body of the e-mail are reformatted, resulting in undesirable changes to the message. Use the body of the e-mail to explain, very briefly, the nature of your attachment.

Use a signature file with every e-mail message so that contact information appears in the message, in case it is printed out; if you send your message to many parties at once, be sure to use the "blind cc" function so that their names remain private (Schindler, 2004).

Never send large attachments such as graphics or photographs by e-mail, unless you have been asked for them (Schindler, 2004). They take too long to download and aggravate reporters. Still, it may be a good idea to assemble some additional information and mention in your press release that it is available on request. You can pull some basics from your press kit, or, if your press kit is on the school's web site, you can simply include a link (for more information about press kits, see page 56). Other useful extras might include images, question-and-answer sheets, pertinent excerpts of speeches and reports, and black-and-white logos or graphics (Hallahan, 1996).

If you send images, they can be black-and-white prints, color transparencies, or high-resolution electronic files in jpeg format that will print at 300 dpi (dots per inch) or higher. If you are uncertain of the resolution of your electronic images or of how to check the resolution, ask a tech-savvy colleague (or even a journalism student) for help. Often digital images are at much lower resolution than is needed for print. Low-resolution images may look great on your computer screen, but they will be blurry or pixilated in print—if printed at all.

Sample Press Release

• • • • • • • • • • • • • • • • • • • •

[letterhead]

Contact: Luis Rodriguez,
Public Information Officer
E-mail: luisr@centraljunior.edu
Phone: (312) 555-5555
Night Line: (312) 555-5555

April 20, 2005
FOR IMMEDIATE RELEASE

CENTRAL JUNIOR HIGH BECOMES COMMUNITY CENTER

CHICAGO, IL, April 20, 2005—Like other schools in inner-city districts throughout the state, Central Junior High has started hosting evening events catering to parents.

"We hope that these events will break the ice and encourage parents to visit the school more often, to see it as a kind of community center," Principal Lin said. "Studies show that students at schools with active parent involvement score

- more -

COMMUNITY CENTER   PAGE TWO

25% higher on standardized tests and are 50% more likely to graduate from high school."

Central Junior High received a state grant in January to fund the events. Recent offerings include tax assistance, chess tournaments, and self-defense classes. All events are scheduled for Tuesdays and Thursdays, at 7:00 p.m. or later, to allow parents to attend after a full work day and dinner with their children.

Local resident Renee Brown atttends with her son Marcus regularly. "Marcus likes studying with the other kids, and I like to visit with other parents."

For more information, call 555-5555, or visit www.centraljunior.edu.

- end -

Crisis Press Releases

In a crisis, the last thing you will have time for is checking the margins of your press release for accuracy, and in truth, the media will not care about formatting under those circumstances. The first crisis press release can announce the situation, provide emergency information, and notify the press and the public of when the next update will be available. Follow-up news releases can provide new information, correct misinformation, and promise further updates.

As soon as possible after a crisis, send press releases to:

- Acknowledge that the event has occurred.

- Disseminate emergency information.

- Alert the media that they will not be allowed on campus.

- State what measures the school will take, as soon as they are known.

- Give date, time, and location of the news conference, if one is warranted.

- Identify who is the media's primary contact for information.

In your announcement of the crisis, avoid any statements about guilt, innocence, or intent. If a death was by firearm, simply state that, rather than referring to a homicide or suicide. Any information on guilt or intent should come from the police, who will conduct their own investigation.

For less urgent press releases, consider including the following elements:

- A statement of regret

- A general description of student reactions

- A report on the school's response

- A report on the school's expression of condolences and other assistance to affected families

- Information on any memorials, vigils, or related activities

- A list of other support activities or meetings planned for parents or the public

- A request for any assistance the press can offer

Sample Crisis Press Release A

●●●●●●●●●●●●●●●●●●●

This is appropriate immediately following a major event that will involve evacuating the school and may attract media attention from outside the community.

[letterhead]

Contact: Richard Kensington,
Public Information Officer
E-mail: rkensington@eisenhowerhigh.edu
Phone: (410) 555-5555
Night Line: (410) 555-5555

April 14, 2005
FOR IMMEDIATE RELEASE

REGARDING THE EVOLVING CRISIS AT EISENHOWER HIGH

SMITHTON, MARYLAND—A critical incident is unfolding at Eisenhower High School. We will give additional updates when we know more. Please share this urgent information with the community as soon as possible:

Shots have been reported at Eisenhower High School. The school is being evacuated, and emergency personnel have been called to the scene. You can help emergency vehicles respond to the crisis by avoiding the following streets:

- more -

EISENHOWER CRISIS   PAGE TWO

- Second Street from Fairfax Avenue to Hillside Avenue

- Oak Street from Second Street to Seventeenth Street

In accordance with district policy, only emergency personnel will be allowed on school grounds at this time.

Students at Eisenhower High are being evacuated to the Miller Convention Center. Parents can pick up their children in the auditorium of the convention center. The school must account for every child leaving the site. Only those who are already on the child's emergency contact list will be allowed to take the child; new contacts cannot be added to the emergency contact list today.

For more information, call 555-1200. That number will be up and running, staffed with knowledgeable people, by noon today. Do **not** call the regular school line, as that line is needed for emergency response. Radio station KBBB and TV station WXFB will carry updates when they are released.

The next news release will be sent within 2 hours when more information becomes available. A news conference is also being planned. Details will be sent to you when they are finalized. Thank you for sharing this information with the public.

— end —

Sample Crisis Press Release B

• • • • • • • • • • • • • • • • • • •

This is appropriate in the days following a major event that may attract media attention from outside the community.

[letterhead]

Contact: Richard Kensington,
Public Information Officer
E-mail: rkensington@eisenhowerhigh.edu
Phone: (410) 555-5555
Night Line: (410) 555-5555

April 18, 2005
FOR IMMEDIATE RELEASE

SCHOOL SHOOTING AT EISENHOWER HIGH

SMITHTON, MARYLAND—The facts are emerging in the days following the school shooting at Eisenhower High School on April, 14, 2005. The police investigation has confirmed that Robert Griggs, a junior at the school, killed two fellow students, Mary Black and Chad Wilson, before killing himself.

Robert Griggs was a junior at Eisenhower High. He was a member of the wrestling team. Mary Black was a sophomore and a member of the girls' volleyball team and the choir. Chad Wilson was a junior and had recently moved to Smithton from Florida, where he had been active in wrestling and in football.

- more -

Media Relations for Schools • Copyright © 2007 by Cheri Lovre
Solution Tree • www.solution-tree.com

EISENHOWER SHOOTING   PAGE TWO

"Police have not determined the cause of Robert Griggs' actions," Principal Michaels stated. "This tragedy has touched many lives at the school, and our thoughts are with the families at this difficult time."

Principal Michaels noted that the Flight Team—trained team members of neighboring schools from within and outside the district—had stepped in to assist Eisenhower staff in the aftermath of the crisis. "Students are respectful and subdued," Michaels said. "The school opened the library for several days as a drop-in center for students to gather, share memories, and grieve together."

Students are planning a memorial event to pay tribute to the lives of the victims to be held at the school on Wednesday, April 20, at noon. Media may attend but may not interview students, parents, or staff at that time and must remain in the area designated for media representatives.

A meeting for parents will be held at City Hall on Friday at 7:00 p.m. to discuss the school's security plan and ways parents can assist children in grief. Principal Michaels, Dr. Ray Toshida, and chief of police Martin Sharp will attend. Media representatives are invited to attend the first half-hour of the meeting; parents will have an opportunity to discuss the tragedy in privacy afterwards.

A news conference for further updates on the crisis is scheduled for Tuesday, April 19, at 9 a.m. at the Miller Convention Center, in the Elm Room.

— end —

Sample Crisis Press Release C

• • • • • • • • • • • • • • • • • •

This is appropriate for an event which touches the lives of many in a community but will not likely draw national media attention.

[letterhead]

Contact: Richard Kensington,
Public Information Officer
E-mail: rkensington@eisenhowerhigh.edu
Phone: (410) 555-5555
Night Line: (410) 555-5555

January 18, 2005
FOR IMMEDIATE RELEASE

SCHOOL RESPONDS TO STUDENT'S DEATH

Yesterday evening, John Smith, a student at Eisenhower High, was killed in an incident involving a firearm. "We are shocked and saddened by John Smith's death," Principal Michaels said, "and extend our condolences to his family. Our vice-principal visited with his family last evening."

John Smith was a junior at Eisenhower. He moved into the district 2 years ago and was active in athletics. John was a member of the FFA group and participated in state fair competitions for show horses.

- more -

STUDENT DEATH   PAGE TWO

The Flight Team, Eisenhower High's crisis response team, has come in to help provide the extra support the school needs at times such as these. "Their presence makes it possible to open extra space for our students to gather and share memories of John," Principal Michaels noted.

The tenor of the school is subdued and respectful. Students are openly grieving and coping as well as one might hope.

Eisenhower High will hold a student-organized gathering on Friday morning in John's memory. "His parents have been invited to attend this fitting tribute to a fine young man," Principal Michaels said. "Our hearts continue to be with the family at this time."

The school will hold a press conference on January 20 at noon at City Hall.

— end —

Notice that Sample Crisis Press Release B does not speculate on why the school shooting occurred. Similarly, in Sample Crisis Press Release C, the first paragraph makes no statement about the nature of the death other than that the cause was known to be a firearm. Any statement about guilt or innocence, intent, suicide, or other issues will appear in the police report. It is in the best interest of the school to not formally discuss those kinds of issues. When the shooting death occurs at home, you may even want to avoid the word "accident." Some argue that any home that contains a firearm (even legally) increases the opportunity for firearm-related deaths, and that these deaths may be unintentional, but not strictly accidental. Community members may become particularly sensitive to language under such stressful circumstances. Using neutral language such as "incident" allows the school to remain outside the circle of debate.

Also notice that there is no connotation that the Flight Team, the crisis response team, is there to help "troubled" students. It is better to indicate that these are exceptionally caring school staff who have had special training in how to facilitate the grief process in the school setting for *all* students. But making too much of the team's professional expertise can sometimes deter students from seeking help; students do not want to be singled out as "troubled" or particularly "needy." If your school creates a special space set aside for students to grieve together (a "Safe Room"), do not refer to it in your press releases by that name. Instead, describe it in general terms as a "place for students to gather" or a "drop-in center." (For more information about general crisis response, see the *Crisis Resource Manual.* For more information about responding to trauma and tragedy, see *The Safe Room: A Guide for School Crisis Responders.*)

Press Release Checklist

_____ Follow the technical format of a press release for margins, spacing, paragraph indents, headers, and footers.

_____ Make sure the spelling and grammar are clean and error-free: Use spell-check and ask someone else to proofread the text.

_____ Capture the key ideas in the headline and lead paragraph using crisp, catchy language.

_____ Write the text in the third person, and organize material clearly and logically.

_____ Ensure that each paragraph focuses on one topic and uses no more than three sentences.

_____ Anticipate—and answer—basic questions readers are likely to have.

_____ Use quotes to advance the story. Clearly identify speakers by name and position.

_____ Check that the story meets at least two definitions of what makes a good story.

_____ Secure the administration's approval on the final draft.

_____ Make a press kit or other additional information available on request.

_____ Use "blind cc" and an appropriate subject line for e-mailed press releases; do not include large attachments.

_____ Keep a record of your contacts and quickly follow up on all requests for additional information.

_____ Check the paper for your story, compare it to the press release, archive a copy of the story, and correct any errors.

Media Advisories

A media advisory (or media alert) serves only one purpose: to summon reporters to a news conference or any other event that you believe the media will want to cover in person (Miller, 2005). If your event or conference does not contain enough information to warrant the reporter's trip to a special site, it should be a press release, not an event. If it does warrant the trip, use a media advisory, not a press release. A press release should only be used to call a news conference when you are in a crisis situation and need to consolidate information to the press in one announcement. Always be sure to secure the approval of your board, principal, or school administration beforehand. Provide them with a copy of the media advisory, the agenda for the event, and the speech you plan to make. Incorporate any changes *before* securing a location and sending out the media advisory.

A media advisory is always headed by "Media Advisory," centered and in a large-point font. It contains six single-spaced paragraphs, one each for sections titled "Who," "What," "Where," "When," "Why," and "Contact." Those titles should appear along the left-hand side of the page in a large-point font (Miller, 2005). A media advisory gets down to business: You do not have to use complete sentences as long as the information is clear. Do not reveal the information that is going to be announced at the news conference or event.

Send your media advisory to a specific person from your media directory, if possible. If you do not know a name, use the appropriate title. At a television station, a media advisory should go to the "assignment editor." If you know a producer at the station by name, copy him or her on the letter. At a radio station, a media advisory should go to the "news director." At a newspaper, a media advisory should go to the "city desk," the editor, and any reporters that you know cover education. Hopefully, you will have already established contacts and will be able to use the correct title and name for each media outlet.

Crisis Media Advisories

In a crisis, it is fine to combine notice of your upcoming news conference with a press release giving general information about the crisis. If you have time and a template ready to make a separate media advisory, however, doing so may be a good way to make sure you have included all of the relevant information.

Sample Media Advisory

[letterhead]

MEDIA ADVISORY

WHO   Principal Judith Rosenberg, together with School Board President Ron Cummings, Mr. and Mrs. John Martin, and Stony Creek High track coach Bill Jones.

WHAT   Stony Creek High School will dedicate the new Angela Martin track field and announce a major new athletics program for girls.

WHERE   The dedication will be made on site, at the south end of the field. Parking will be available in the south lot behind the high school. Note: No electric power is available on site.

WHEN   Wednesday, September 14, at 11:00 a.m. The press conference will begin promptly. Principal Rosenberg and Mr. and Mrs. Martin will be available for live TV and radio interviews beginning at about noon.

WHY   Former student Angela Martin, 1999 state champion in class A track, was killed in an auto accident on her way to an Olympic training camp last year. This press conference will explain a new athletics program founded in her honor.

CONTACT Genessee County District Schools public information office: Victoria Smith, Public Information Officer, or Debbie White, Assistant Public Information Officer, at 917-555-5555.

Sample Crisis Media Advisory

```
                    [letterhead]

                  MEDIA ADVISORY

WHO      Principal Judith Rosenberg, Stony Creek
         High School; Chief James Wosniewski,
         Smithton Police Department; School Board
         President Ron Cummings.

WHAT     Principal Rosenberg and Chief Wosniewski
         will discuss the school shooting that
         occurred on Monday, September 12.

WHERE    The Oak Room, Holiday Inn at I-70 and
         South Smith Road.

WHEN     Wednesday, September 14, at 11:00 a.m.
         The press conference will begin
         promptly.

WHY      Principal Rosenberg and Chief Wosniewski
         will give updates in the investigation
         and crisis response. Maria Espinoza of
         the Red Cross will provide the
         perspectives of the agencies
         coordinating the emergency response
         efforts.

CONTACT  Genessee County District Schools public
         information office: Victoria Smith,
         Public Information Officer, or Debbie
         White, Assistant Public Information
         Officer, at 917-555-5555.
```

Media Advisory Checklist

____ Check that the event's purpose cannot be met by a press release and that reporters must be there in person to get the full story.

____ Secure approval from the principal and school administration to hold a news event, and review the materials to be covered with them.

____ Include the 5 Ws and contact information in the media advisory.

____ Ensure that spelling is correct.

____ Double-check the time, date, and place to be sure they are accurate.

____ Keep a record of your contacts and their responses to the media advisory.

Media Relations for Schools • Copyright © 2007 by Cheri Lovre
Solution Tree • www.solution-tree.com

News Conferences

A news conference is a live event in which the media is invited to hear one or more speakers discuss an event or situation. It is a way to reach many reporters at once with critical, time-sensitive information and to provide them with controlled access to people who can answer questions. News conferences may be an important part of media relations during a crisis that attracts national attention, or even during a lesser crisis in a metropolitan area with many news outlets. You should only call a news conference if three conditions are met (Schiller, 2004):

1. Reporters need to ask questions and take photographs;

2. Many reporters need this contact (too many to hold separate interviews); and

3. The information is urgently needed.

A news conference has two significant elements: a prepared opening speech and a question-and-answer period. It may also include statements from other parties or visual aids of some kind. The opening speech should be 3–5 minutes long and *full of short, simple "sound bites."* When writing your speech, think about its key topics (both positive and negative), and identify two or three points you want to make about each topic. Reduce each point down to 100 words or less, and then further reduce each point to create 5- to 15-second sound bites for television and radio (Czarnecki, 2005). Practice reading your speech out loud; be sure that it is easy to read in 3–5 minutes.

Consider what kinds of questions reporters might ask, and write out your responses in question-and-answer format (later, you can include this sheet as part of the materials distributed at the conference). Reiterate your main points in your responses, and *practice saying them out loud*. Be sure to include the questions you most dread in your practice draft, so that you will be prepared for the worst; you do not have to include those in the public version of the question-and-answer sheet.

Finally, create a written version of your statement that can be approved by your principal, school board, or both *before* the conference (along with any other printed materials you will be distributing). Adjust it to reflect any of their comments before copying it to distribute to reporters.

When planning the actual event, choose a neutral location away from the school, with room for all of the attendees inside and plenty of parking outside. City hall or the public library may have an auditorium you can use. If audiovisual equipment is available on site or through a rental company, that may be helpful, but many news teams now are geared for wireless transmission. The least you will require is a speaker's dais and a microphone. Audio feed boxes and flood lights are also helpful.

A news conference needs to be early in the day—for instance, at 10:00 a.m.—so that reporters have time to organize and edit the information before their afternoon deadlines. If you are on the West Coast and your situation will attract national media attention, remember that with the time difference, East Coast deadlines will be even earlier.

A news conference has a much more professional quality in the right setting. The speaker's lectern should be on a raised platform. If you have multiple speakers, use a table with a mike for every speaker. Do not leave the background blank: Use plants, flags, or curtains to add interest for photographs and video. Make sure speakers are dressed in appropriate business attire. Men should wear a dark suit and a bold but simple tie with no busy patterns. For women, a solid-colored dress or suit in a strong color is best. Avoid stripes, busy patterns, and shiny materials. Do not wear jewelry that moves, makes noise, glitters, or otherwise distracts (International Competition Network, 2005).

If you are using audiovisual equipment, set up tables along one side of the room for audio feedboxes that reporters can plug into to record the audio portion. Set an additional audio feedbox on the floor at the back of the room for television crews. If you can, use flood lights to provide front and back lighting for the speaker, to make it easier for video crews and to eliminate distracting flash photography (Schiller, 2004).

Chairs for the reporters should be arranged in one central block, very close to the platform. Do not create a central aisle; the purpose of the block arrangement is to allow photographers to shoot from the sides and video crews to shoot from the back without blocking anyone's view of the speaker (Schiller, 2004).

Set up a table at the door with neat stacks of media kits and a press sign-in sheet. Assign someone to greet media representatives, ask them to sign in or leave a card, and distribute media kits. If a reporter refuses to sign in or leave a card, he or she should still receive a media kit. If a reporter wants to take the media kit and leave, that is okay, too—the media kit should contain the full text of any prepared remarks, fact sheets, background information, and possibly a photo and bio of the speaker (Schiller, 2004).

Public Speaking 101

- Know who will be in the room and what you want them to know.

- Type out your speech on index cards or the top third of a page, so that you will not have to look down.

- Practice giving your speech.

- Time your practice run (a 10-minute talk is 1,600–1,800 words).

- For important speeches, record yourself on a practice run.

- Breathe deeply and stretch for a few minutes prior to your speech.

- Smile and make eye contact.

- Use a clear, slow, strong voice—Don't rush yourself.

- Slide pages rather than turning them to make less noise in the microphone.

- Stand straight. Do not lean on the podium or shift your weight from foot to foot.

- Keep your feet about 12 inches apart, with one leg slightly forward.

- Keep one arm bent at the elbow and use hand gestures.

- If you use a chart or other visual, point to it, but do not leave the microphone.

- Credit your sources.

- Thank the audience at the beginning and the end.

(Adapted from Czarnecki, 2005, and International Competition Network, 2005)

When the appointed time for the press conference arrives, have someone (perhaps the greeter) introduce the speaker. The speaker should not be in the room before the conference, or reporters may start asking questions too soon. The speaker begins by thanking attendees and makes some opening remarks (the 3- to 5-minute speech). The speaker then takes questions by calling on and pointing to reporters on both sides of the room (Schiller, 2004).

You can allow each reporter one follow-up question, if needed, by calling on him or her again. Maintain eye contact as you reply to questions, and if a reporter's voice is too quiet, repeat the question for the room before answering. Stay on topic: Repeat your rehearsed main points as often as possible, in short sound bites.

Remember, you have control. You indicate when your response is complete by calling on the next person, and you indicate when the question-and-answer period is complete by saying, "We have time for one more question" (or "a few more questions"). Do not end during a heated exchange, and always thank everyone again for attending (International Competition Network, 2005).

Often reporters will wait until the press conference is over to ask their best questions. Each reporter wants a statement different from those that other stations or newspapers have. Be patient and answer as many questions as you can. Remain friendly and relaxed.

Sample News Conference Agenda

● ● ● ● ● ● ● ● ● ● ● ● ● ● ● ● ● ● ● ●

[letterhead]

News Conference Agenda

October 10, 2005

City Hall, Rosa Parks Room 204, San Diego, CA

9:00-9:05 a.m.   Introduction by Principal
                   Woods, San Diego Junior High

9:05-9:15 a.m.   Statement by Michelle
                   Martinez, chair of the county
                   school board: The status of
                   redistricting

9:15-9:45 a.m.   Question-and-answer period

Answering Tricky Questions

If you do not know the answer, say that you will find out and respond later.

We're still verifying that information. I'll contact you as soon as it is confirmed.

Do not disclose confidential information, but explain why you cannot do so.

District policy prevents me from commenting on personnel issues.

Respond to negative questions or issues *(Why are test scores so low?)* with a positive answer.

We are working to improve test scores. Our teachers have just spent 2 weeks in an intensive training program for helping children at risk meet the challenges of standardized testing.

If a question is unclear, respond to the most obvious interpretation. Do not ask the reporter to reword it—you will appear evasive.

Respond to aggressive third-party quotes *(John Smith said this administration's approach to school violence is inexcusably negligent),* but do not address the third party in any way. Use first person or passive voice, and weave in your key message.

Our new violence-prevention plan is based on proven research. Student reports of bullying are down by 20% after just 3 weeks.

Do not take the bait with "either/or" questions *(Either you haven't done the research, or the administration is lying to the public).* Find a third way.

This is a complex issue. We're still learning what is most effective for our community's children.

Interviewing 101

In general:

- Nothing is ever "off the record." Assume the tape is always rolling.

- Treat all reporters with respect and courtesy—even those who are rude to you.

- Speak slowly and distinctly. Avoid legal or technical jargon.

- Redirect tricky questions. Never say, "No comment."

- Be succinct: When you have made your point, stop talking.

- Thank the reporter at the beginning and the end of the interview.

On television:

- Do not wear any jewelry that is shiny, noisy, or moves. Choose solid-colored business attire.

- Do not look into the camera. Maintain eye contact with the reporter.

- When sitting, clasp your hands on a desk or in your lap, with your arms loose.

- Keep your body still, but move your head; be expressive with your face and voice.

(continued)

Crisis News Conferences

In a crisis, being familiar with the procedures of a news conference will be invaluable. Reporters will ask some of their toughest questions, and the pressure of media attention will be at its most intense. Even as the crisis winds down, you may be in demand for one-on-one interviews.

Interviewing 101 (continued)

- Do not lick your lips, squint, roll your eyes, scratch your head, point at the reporter, or blink or sigh excessively.

- Pause after significant statements and sound bites to allow the editors to cut the film to highlight the pertinent parts of the interview later.

On the radio:

- Hold your head steady to maintain the same distance from the microphone.

- Do not try to fill awkward silences with idle chat or humor. Let the host fill empty airtime.

- Wait until you are ready to speak so that you do not have to fill in with "er" and "um."

In person or over the phone:

- Allow reporters to record, and speak at your normal volume.

- Do not quote statistics—but be prepared to give a handout or send an e-mail with confirmed data.

- Nothing is ever "off the record." Assume the tape is always rolling.

(Adapted from Schiller, 2004)

When possible, hold joint news conferences with other stakeholders in the crisis: emergency services, police, or hospital staff (for more information on coordinating content, see Planning for Effective Media Relations, page 63). In addition to confirming the content with your administration, be sure that any families involved in the crisis, your police liaison, and others who will be affected know the content of any statements before they are released to the media. For your oral statement, treat it as if it were written: Remember, you will be distributing copies of it. Follow the model of the crisis press release. Include:

- A brief acknowledgment of the significance of the event to students and staff

- Basic student data (such as how long the student has been at the school or what activities he or she participated in, if appropriate)

- Confirmation of the event as you know it, referring any questions in the domain of the police, district attorney, hospital, or other agencies to them for an answer

- A brief statement on how the students, staff, and crisis response team are reacting

- News, if known, of any planned memorial activity and the students' participation in the planning

- An invitation to ask questions

News Conference Checklist

•••••••••••••••••••

Before the conference

____ Select and prepare speakers on content, procedure, and what to wear.

____ Reserve the room, furnishings, equipment, and technical crew (if necessary).

____ Send the media advisory.

____ Prepare written statements, an agenda, and a media sign-in sheet.

____ Assemble enough media packets for all those invited.

____ Assign people to staff the media table, to introduce the speaker, to take notes, and to record the conference.

During the conference

____ Check that all speakers are present and ready and that electrical equipment is working.

____ Monitor the sign-in sheet, and distribute press kits.

____ Thank the audience for their attendance.

____ Call on reporters from both sides of the room.

____ Allow for follow-up questions.

____ Stay cordial, and redirect tough questions.

____ Check that notes are being taken and the proceedings recorded.

After the conference

____ Return props and put the room back to its original order.

____ Debrief speakers.

____ Call reporters with follow-up answers.

____ Track and clip or record news coverage of the conference.

____ Correct inaccurate coverage.

Press Kits

A press kit is a file of background information that reporters can consult to round out their stories. A press kit is the same whether it is used in regular or in crisis media relations; once it is prepared, it is available at any time.

For schools, a press kit might include school history, enrollment and demographic figures, milestones, growth, curriculum development, a map, copies of prior news stories about the school, names and vitas of administrators, and photos. Each page should contain the name of the school or district, its web site, and a contact name, phone number, and e-mail address in the header or footer. Keep individual documents short, to one page if possible.

An electronic file with high-resolution images suitable for print (300 dpi or above, in jpeg or tiff format) is best as it can be easily duplicated and sent via e-mail—or, even better, posted on the school or district web site for downloading (for more information about technical issues with digital files, see page 26). If you post your press kit online, make it easy to find on the site, and do not require a password to access it (Schindler, 2004). Make sure the images you include are print-ready (not web-resolution bitmaps), and if possible, include links to past and current press releases.

If you keep a hardcopy file, keep a separate file for originals (of maps and photos, for example), and maintain at least three copies of the press kit on hand at any time.

Remember to update your press kit. Administrators and demographics change, and your press kit should change with them. This information will be helpful year-round to reporters looking for extra detail for their stories. In a crisis, it will give them material to work with early on, when you might not have the time to give them a complete story.

Sample School History

● ● ● ● ● ● ● ● ● ● ● ● ● ● ● ● ● ● ● ●

[letterhead]

Contact: Frank Smith, Public Information Officer
E-mail: franksmith@wshton.edu
Phone: (555) 555-1212

WASHINGTON HIGH SCHOOL HISTORY

Washington High was designed by George Raymond, a prominent architect of the mid-century, and built in 1956. The original site purchased by the district included 40 acres of adjacent farmland. Plans called for locally quarried limestone to be used surrounding the main entry and carved into Raymond's signature herringbone pattern, which is also featured on the county courthouse.

In 1969, the district sold 10 acres from the original parcel back to the city. The city turned that 10 acres into Westside Park in the early 1970s.

The Davis Athletic Field was added in 1978 and named in memory of Washington High's first principal, Robert Davis.

In 1982, the Washington High Panthers, the girls' basketball team, won their first of three consecutive state championships. The Panthers were also state champions in 1994, 1997, and 2003.

- more -

WASHINGTON HIGH SCHOOL HISTORY   PAGE TWO

By 1984, the district's population had tripled since 1956, and Washington High began extensive renovations. Architects Rogers and Lee designed a new wing equal in size to the existing building, and contractors Klein, Johnston, and Schmidt began construction in September. The original limestone entry was retained for its historic value to the community.

In 1985, Washington High became the magnet school for science in Greene County, and the Whitney Science Center, part of the ongoing renovation, was completed with a federal grant.

In 2001, Washington High began revising its curriculum to become a professional learning community.

In 2004, the state awarded Washington High "most improved" status.

— end —

Sample School Fact Sheet

● ● ● ● ● ● ● ● ● ● ● ● ● ● ● ● ● ● ●

[letterhead]

Contact: Frank Smith, Public Information Officer
E-mail: franksmith@wshton.edu
Phone: (555) 555-1212

WASHINGTON HIGH SCHOOL FACT SHEET

- Washington High School (est. 1956) currently has enrollment of 3,454 and is the largest high school in Greene County.

- Washington High's student population is 65% African American, 20% Hispanic, 10% Caucasian, 1% Asian American, and 4% other.

- 72% of Washington students live in families that meet government standards for poverty.

- 85% of Washington students complete high school; 45% of Washington students go on to college.

- Since 2000, Washington students have consistently scored in the 85th percentile or higher in standardized state testing.

- In 2005, Washington High students averaged 1100 on the SAT. Two students were finalists for National Merit Scholarships.

- more -

WASHINGTON HIGH SCHOOL FACT SHEET   PAGE TWO

- Washington High's girls' basketball team, the Panthers, is a six-time state champion in the class B division. In 2003, the team placed third in national competition.

- Prominent graduates of Washington High include singer LeShaun Broyer (class of '98), State District Attorney Phil Byrd (class of '75), and the president and founder of MicroTech Medical, Jon Cardenas (class of '80).

— end —

Press Kit Checklist

• • • • • • • • • • • • • • • • • • • •

_____ Include a short school history and a fact sheet with current enrollment figures and demographics, using bulleted lists or short, three-sentence paragraphs.

_____ Include a list of administrative and other priority figures (team coaches, program directors, and so on), along with pertinent biographical detail.

_____ Include several images, including photographs of the school (and any special facilities or athletic fields) and of key administrators and faculty members.

_____ For digital images, include only high-resolution jpegs or tiffs.

_____ Obtain administrative approval on all items in the press kit.

_____ Include the school or district's name and a contact name, phone number, and e-mail on every sheet.

_____ Create an easy-to-find online version that does not require a password or prior authorization to download.

_____ Add links to past and current press releases to the online version.

Media Relations for Schools • Copyright © 2007 by Cheri Lovre
Solution Tree • www.solution-tree.com

Chapter 3

Planning for Effective Media Relations

PLANNING

The media tools discussed in the previous chapter are most effective when they are used as part of a detailed media relations plan. Media relations planning results in:

- A clear policy

- A written media plan that addresses both ongoing and crisis media relations

- A formal outline of media roles and responsibilities for each team member

- A set of media resources that can aid the communications team

- Training and practice for the communications team

Materials should be stored in a location that is easily accessible throughout the year and in a crisis (keeping in mind that the school may have to be evacuated). Keep duplicates in two other locations, such as the nearest school and the district office. All materials should be updated regularly. Refresher training courses can also be helpful.

Set Policy

The first step in planning for positive, proactive media relations is to establish district policies and procedures for everyday issues and crisis situations. Being prepared allows the school and district to be seen as organized, capable, and credible. It fosters better cooperation from media year-round and gives you an edge of authority from media and from participating response agencies in a crisis.

If such policies are not already in place in your district, take steps to develop communications policies and procedures. Even a small district with limited resources should take time to outline a crisis plan to provide the media and the public with timely and appropriate information in emergency situations. In a large district, the sheer number of constituents and administrators requires clarifying exactly who will do what, and when. It is important to make sure that people know their responsibilities—that they do not assume someone else is taking care of the details. In a crisis, you will not have time to learn how to navigate a complex bureaucracy, so plan ahead.

Bring up the issue of media relations, including crisis response, at an administrators' meeting. If there is no district-wide policy to support the media relations efforts of school administrators, get consensus on the need to have one, particularly in times of crisis. Consider creating a subcommittee to provide recommendations. Keep working on that task until a district-wide policy is in place. Because schools are public buildings, they may be subject to special restrictions or liabilities: Have your final policy reviewed by the district's attorney.

Articulate Philosophy and Priorities

Consider including the following general points as part of your district's media relations policy. You may need to adjust these or add to them in order to address your district's particular situation and needs.

1. The district and school's primary responsibility is to students, staff, and their families. All media relations should be based on how to better serve the needs of students and staff. You may want to identify and prioritize those needs before outlining what part media relations can play in meeting them on an ongoing basis and during a crisis.

2. The press has a role within the community and a right to their story; the school will provide a prompt and accurate response to media. In order to respond to media needs—or, even better, to proactively address them—identify who will assume responsibility for media communications. There are many ways to share information, as shown in the previous chapter: press kits, web sites, e-mail, faxes, press releases, phone calls, interviews, and news conferences.

Especially in a crisis, the school and district should be willing to supply adequate information to the news media, as long as it can be done without changing the quality and efficacy of the crisis response efforts. Because reporters will want to interview administrators and other school figures—key people who have more pressing obligations—it is very important to establish one person, a public information officer, who can speak on their behalf. Doing so will make a big difference in the quality of news coverage and, more importantly, the effectiveness of crisis management.

3.   In the interest of generating goodwill with the media and creating a positive public image, administrators and public information officers would do well to become familiar with media organizations, their protocol, and their deadlines. Knowing who to contact, when and how to contact them, and having established personal working relations with local reporters will bring the district credibility and enhance public relations. It may also encourage the media to cooperate when a crisis does occur.

4.   During a crisis, news conferences and interviews will always be held off site. You will provide students, staff, and parents with much more protection and privacy if you interact with reporters at a site not related to the district. During a crisis, keeping media representatives away from school property and from any evacuation site will protect your students and staff. By holding news conferences at a location away from the school and the crisis zone, you can provide as much of the story as you like without jeopardizing the needs of students and staff for privacy during the grieving process. Set policy on this, and identify off-site locations that may meet your needs. Meeting with reporters off site on a regular basis may make this approach more acceptable and familiar to them during a crisis.

5. In a crisis situation, no one but emergency workers can come onto school grounds without specific invitation from the principal or site administrator. Waiting to make decisions about media presence until the day of crisis makes it nearly impossible to handle media relations well. Institute a "no trespass" policy to keep media as well as others away from the school *before* crisis strikes. A no-trespass policy protects students and staff from media presence and keeps reporters and others from tainting the scene of the investigation. It also gives you a way to restrict parental access, if necessary. The school can invite the media to specific events—a memorial event, for example—but restrict them from having free access to the school building. The school can thus preserve a modicum of control over what the media observes and reports about how the tragedy is being handled. Short of state law limiting media access to crises (like the one Arizona has), having district-wide policies in place (rather than individual school policies) is best.

Although reporters may claim that since a school is a public building, the media have access rights, it is possible to enact and justify a no-trespass policy. Principals have the right and responsibility to protect the school site because their primary responsibility is assuring student safety and well-being. To sidestep the potential label of "obstructionist," however, the district should complement its no-trespass policy with other policies that clearly outline how the district will accommodate media, parents, and other potential visitors. Encourage reporters to tape file footage when the school is not in crisis, so that in a news-worthy tragedy, reporters will have something on hand to roll immediately. File footage can provide a cushion of time before reporters come onto school grounds.

6. After a traumatic event, students need the opportunity to grieve and express their fears at school and out of the public eye. Even if the death or critical event did not occur at school, if the school setting was the environment in which students knew the affected people, there will be a reaction within the school setting. Grief has a social component that is environment-specific. Students need time and space to respond to grief, without media presence.

7. A family's dignity and integrity call for a sense of privacy. If you could speak with nearly any family who has had a loved one die in a high-interest or sensational event, you would find that protecting their sense of privacy was often a greater challenge than coping with grief. The district can use its PIO to assist a grieving family by educating them in the basics of media relations, serving as a spokesperson for the family at news conferences, distributing the family's preferred photographs of the child to the press, and respecting, in its own comments, the family's public position on a death with an element of controversy (such as a death by suicide or a death involving drugs or alcohol).

Putting these kinds of stated priorities into a site-specific action plan gives the public information officer a secure administrative base and an explicit rationale to guide his or her media relations. Following policy allows the PIO to build relationships and skills that will be crucial throughout the year and especially when put to the test in a crisis.

Create a Media Plan

Your media relations plan should include two elements: a goal-oriented ongoing plan and a site-specific crisis plan.

The Goal-Oriented Ongoing Plan

Your ongoing plan may be fairly simple or quite complex, depending on the size of your school or district, its needs, and its current relationship with the community. A basic plan should answer the following questions:

- Who is responsible for media relations?

- What tasks are assigned to each position involved with media relations?

- What is the chain of command for approving media materials?

- What are the general guidelines for coverage (what subjects are "off limits")?

- What are the specific goals and priorities for news coverage?

- What is the timeline for reaching media relations goals?

- What benchmarks will be used to evaluate the success of media relations?

Remember to make your goals SMART (O'Neill & Conzemius, 2006): strategic and specific, measurable, attainable, results-oriented, and time-bound. Your priorities might include, for example, a statement such as, "We will publicize our three core after-school programs in reading, math, and life skills to increase enrollment and community participation." To further the effectiveness of your media relations plan, you might then specify, "We will publicize our three core programs with at least one story a month for 6 months; our first coverage will be achieved by October 10." Benchmarks for measuring your success could include a 20% increase in student enrollment, a 25% increase in adult volunteers staffing the programs, or recruiting two new partners in the business community to underwrite the cost of materials. Look for ways to correlate achievements to publicity. For instance, consider creating a form to track how many new enrollees or volunteers learned about the program from the newspaper or television coverage.

Media relations alone may not accomplish your goals, of course, but they can play a significant role in achieving them. You may get a spontaneous outpouring of support after an article appears, or you may not hear a peep from anyone. Regardless of the response from the public to media coverage, your letters to parents and businesspeople recruiting their support can refer to that coverage to prove how valuable the programs are.

For small schools with limited staff and resources, remember that you can ask school board members, parent volunteers, and PTA officers to assist with some tasks or to support the media campaign through letters to the editor, either before or after an article appears. An administrator's thank-you letter that mentions how hard teachers are working to improve test scores in the district, a teacher's letter that explains other program benefits not mentioned in the article, a parent's letter that testifies to the program's effectiveness—these may not carry the authority of the newspaper's own coverage, but they still reach a wide readership and affect the public's perception. If you do involve others in a support campaign, ask if it would be possible to receive a copy of the letter before it appears in the paper, and be sure to thank all letter writers profusely for their time and efforts.

> ## Elements of a Successful Ongoing Media Relations Campaign
>
> • A district-wide policy of positive media relations
>
> • Thoroughly trained media relations staff and volunteers
>
> • Support and accessibility of administration to approve materials
>
> • Goals that are strategic and specific, measurable, attainable, results-oriented, and time-bound
>
> • The ability of the PIO and media staff to earn the respect and cooperation of media

The Site-Specific Crisis Plan

The second element of a media relations plan focuses on crisis communications. In a crisis, the regular channels for communication may not be open, and administration and staff will be overwhelmed with other critical tasks (see the *Crisis Resource Manual*). The district should develop a detailed communications plan that allows for quick response to media as a crisis unfolds. Clear, precise plans lay the groundwork for acting with confidence and authority to achieve the best results for your school and the community.

Before developing your crisis communications plan, check with other local government agencies (the mayor or city manager's office, county commissioners' offices, or other school districts) to review their emergency communications plans. Avoid duplicating services: Build your plan in a collaborative fashion with those who will also be mobilized to respond to catastrophic events (for more information on crisis response planning, please see the *Crisis Resource Manual* and the *Catastrophic Events Resource Manual*).

Many districts have based their crisis response plans on the National Incident Management System (NIMS) developed by the Federal Emergency Management Agency (FEMA). Perhaps a better approach would be to learn about the NIMS plan and see how your district fits within your city and county plans. Most of the elements crucial for responding to school-based crises are not covered by the NIMS system. NIMS is designed to clarify and empower the agency responsible for the overall crisis response: That hierarchy is important for administrators to know and understand. Schools have other responsibilities, however, including all of the human-related components of reuniting students with parents, providing follow-up support to students, and in general overseeing the well-being and recovery of staff, students, and families. All of that requires work outside the scope of NIMS.

Nevertheless, in a catastrophic event that affects your whole community, you will be bound by the NIMS chain of command. If the police take control of your building, for example, you will not be able to re-enter the building to get your computer, car keys, attendance records, media directory and sample press releases, or anything else. Prepare for that possibility; keep copies of your crisis media relations plan and any supporting records accessible off site.

At its most basic, your crisis media relations plan should answer these questions:

- Who will be the PIO or media liaison?

- What role will district administrators have?

- Where could the crisis communications center, news conferences, and rumor control be located?

- Who will meet with media representatives at a news conference on crisis day?

- What student information will always be given (as part of the public record)?

- What might a crisis news statement include?

Elements of a Successful Crisis Communications Campaign

- Existence of an overall crisis plan as well as a crisis media relations plan

- Pre-established, solid media relations

- Thoroughly trained school staff and team members

- Continuous coordination between PIOs in other crisis response agencies and organizations

- Ability of the lead crisis communications PIO to earn the respect and cooperation of media

---

Educate administration, staff, students, families, and emergency response agencies and organizations on your media plan. Consider, for example, sharing the plan—and their possible roles—with students and staff as part of their orientation for a new school year.

Form Teams

Your media relations plan should clearly define the standard communications team and the crisis communications team: key roles, responsibilities, procedures, contingency plans, and backup personnel.

Standard Communications Team

Your standard communications team will depend on the size of your district and its needs as outlined in your media policy and plan. The team might include the public information officer (for the school or the district), clerical support (existing staff or parent volunteers), and designated "story feeders" among teachers, staff, and possibly even students, who identify and report story ideas to the PIO on a regular basis.

In a large school or district, the PIO and support staff may be full-time employees dedicated to media relations. In a small school or district, the "team" might consist of just one or two people willing to commit to occasional but regular duties: maintaining a current and accurate directory of media contacts, becoming familiar with the tools and guidelines of communicating with the media, and sending out press releases on priority topics on a scheduled (even if infrequent) basis. Your team should be adequately staffed, supported, and funded to meet your media goals. If you cannot provide staff, support, or funds for your media goals, identify those few critical goals that can be achieved with your resources.

The Crisis Communications Team

The crisis communications team should be organized from those who agree to the task and who agree to be trained accordingly. The PIO and other members of the standard communications team, who have established relationships with the media and familiarity with media tools, are essential. Other key members would include PIOs or their designees from:

- The district (if separate from the school PIO)
- The city
- Emergency response agencies
- County emergency services
- FEMA (Federal Emergency Management Agency)
- Red Cross
- Hospital(s)
- County mental health organizations
- The district attorney (school and/or city)
- All others who might benefit by uniting in a collaborative effort

Journalism and speech teachers might be ideal members to consider for the team, provided they are trained in crisis communication and district protocol in advance. Elected officials can make excellent spokespersons if a crisis generates response from a lot of media, especially since the principal will be too busy to be part of the crisis communications team (though he or she should check in frequently). Because there will inevitably be team members absent on any given day, having a number of trained team substitutes is highly advisable.

The crisis communications team will need a home base, a *crisis communications center (CCC)*. Depending on the space available, the CCC may be housed at or near the place serving as the main emergency operations center (which oversees all aspects of the crisis response). To preserve evidence, to keep the crisis site accessible to emergency personnel, and to shield students and staff from the constant barrage of media, the crisis communications center should never be in the school itself or in any other school district office.

Key Roles to Consider

Many of these roles may overlap or require multiple staff members, depending on the size of your district. In some districts, all of these roles will be assumed by one or two people. Be sure to list all roles in an appendix to your media plan. List the name of the person assuming the role (and, for crisis roles, a backup person) and complete contact information. The main roles to consider are as follows:

- Public information officer

- Writer

- Web master

- Record-keeper

- Rumor control

- Note-taker

- Crisis phone bank coordinator and volunteers

- Media compiler

- Go-fer

The **public information officer** handles public relations for the school year-round and during a crisis. In huge metropolitan districts, the central office often hires someone specifically to deal with media and public relations; he or she may handle both internal and external communications. In smaller districts, being PIO may be an auxiliary role for someone already employed in another capacity within the school.

In a crisis, the person who handles media relations is often simply the site administrator of the building where the incident occurred. It is more convenient, however, to have a different person serve as PIO, so that the building administrator can remain free to deal with the crisis at hand. Your superintendent or the proper district authority can facilitate this process by assigning one person on staff to be the public information officer, or PIO. Your district may, in fact, already have a PIO who can help you by serving as a liaison with the press. Learn about your district's existing media relations personnel, and determine who will serve as PIO for your school throughout the year and during a crisis.

The **writer** creates news releases, agendas, and other media relations tools. This may be the PIO or a second person. If the

PIO is also the writer, be sure to have an English teacher or someone else proofread written materials for grammar, clarity, and typos. In larger districts, the writer may also write statements given at news conferences, handouts for staff and parents, newsletter articles, and much more.

The **web master** can assist the PIO by posting a press kit to the school's web site and creating a place on the site where emergency information and updates can be posted in a crisis. Your school or district may already have someone assigned to keep the web site up to date. Learn who that person is, or assign someone if necessary.

The **record-keeper** maintains up-to-date directories of contacts (emergency, administration, media) and keeps files of all press materials generated as well as any responses.

The person in charge of **rumor control** serves as a clearinghouse for all information from staff and students that has not been verified. For example, when a student speaks in class about something that may well be a rumor, the teacher can respond, "Mrs. Jones in Principal Edward's office is taking notes on all rumors and will verify that information and get back to us." This gives teachers a way of asking students not to repeat hearsay, while also giving students a sense of importance when they report what they know to the office for verification. Once the rumors are passed on to the PIO, he or she can then craft messages to help defuse rumors and promote the facts.

The **note-taker** attends all meetings with the PIO and records what has been discussed and decided. It is important that this person be able to quickly and accurately take down comments in a setting with multiple participants.

The **crisis phone bank coordinator and volunteers** are a critical part of the communications team. During a crisis, school phone lines will be overwhelmed by calls. You will need calm, sensible people to answer phones and refer calls. Identify at least a dozen people that might be available to work the phones.

The **media compiler** keeps track and makes copies of news coverage from all sources for future reference. This is a good role for a parent volunteer or a retired person: someone who tends to be around home and has a VCR or DVD recorder. Those responding to a crisis do not have time to watch the news but may need to know what has been reported, particularly after a news conference.

The **go-fer** holds a small but crucial position. There are many small jobs—getting office supplies, snacks, making deliveries—that will need to be done in a crisis. Assign several possible volunteers (perhaps parents) to help with these details.

Identify, Assemble, and Create Resources

Having accurate and complete resources at hand makes using the media on a regular basis much easier, especially for PIOs who hold other positions within the district or school. In a crisis, having all the information handy in a centralized location saves time and possibly lives.

Once you have created the basic resources, be sure to keep them up to date. Scheduling the update for a regular time, such as the third Tuesday of every month, keeps the work of updating simple. Use the header or footer to note the last time the file was updated. Keep contact lists and forms brief, in quick-copy, easy-to-read formats. These should be attached as an appendix to your plan.

The main tasks are as follows:

- Create and maintain an emergency directory.
- Create and maintain an organizational chart and directory.
- Create and maintain a media directory.
- Create and maintain a volunteer staff directory.
- Create media tools templates.
- Assemble a press kit.
- Create or update the school web site.
- Identify, assemble, and create other resources for use in a crisis.
- Identify possible locations for a news conference.
- Identify possible locations for a crisis communications center.
- Research phone lines.

Create and Maintain an Emergency Directory

Ideally, your overall crisis response plan would include an emergency directory. This directory should also be included with your crisis media relations plan. Make a list of phone and fax numbers for police, fire, hospitals, Red Cross, mental health, and other emergency response agencies in the city and county. Many of these agencies will have back lines used by their staff; be sure to ask for these numbers, since 911 and other main lines and listed numbers are likely to be jammed during a crisis.

Create and Maintain an Organizational Chart and Directory

Each school or district should create and maintain an organizational chart listing school officials, public information officers, and key agencies involved in regular and crisis communications, along with the contact information for each. This is helpful not only for making quick contact at any time, but also for answering media questions about school hierarchy.

Create and Maintain a Media Directory

Each school or district should maintain a directory of local media contacts. If one is not currently in place, someone should be appointed to develop and update the list every 3 months. Positions and personnel can change frequently at media outlets, so keeping the directory current is both essential and challenging. Ideally, the person using the directory to send press releases and so on during regular media relations would keep it updated.

The directory should include names, phone and fax numbers, and e-mail addresses for news editors and reporters involved with regular school issues. The directory should indicate each contact's preferred method of contact for press releases (some prefer e-mail to faxes). It should also contain a crisis media contact sheet that accurately indicates at a glance which newspapers and television and radio stations you will probably want to interact with during crises, who in each news organization to contact, and how to reach them. A computerized database is best as it gives you the ability to broadcast news releases to all sources at once, either as a fax or as an e-mail. A hard copy is handy as well; keep it in an off-site location, in case you are forced to evacuate the school.

Create and Maintain a Volunteer Staff Directory

Using the team roles outlined in your plan, create a directory of all auxiliary media relations staff who might need to be called in a crisis. This could include phone bank staff, go-fers, and others who are able and trained to assist in an emergency.

Create Media Tools Templates

Using the information and samples from chapter 2 (included on the CD at the back of this book), create templates for press releases, media alerts, and news conference agendas. Store the templates on a computer so that it is easy for the PIO or press liaison to fill out a correctly formatted press release or agenda on a regular basis. Keep samples, checklists, and a copy of the media directory in the same folder.

Create a sample crisis press release that can be filled at a moment's notice, to cover any number of emergency events, and faxed or e-mailed in the immediate aftermath. Create a sample crisis news conference agenda as well.

Assemble a Press Kit

Using the information and examples from chapter 2 (included on the CD at the back of this book), create fact sheets that reporters can use to fill out their stories. Remember to create a routine schedule for updating the press kit and to assign that duty to one person.

Create or Update the School Web Site

If your school or district has a web site, consider adding a downloadable press kit and a page designated to hold emergency information. In a crisis, you can use that space to give information to parents and the media, to provide updates on the school's crisis response, and to link to other sites that may have important emergency or prevention information.

Identify, Assemble, and Create Other Resources for Use in a Crisis

In an emergency, the crisis response team may need to create written materials such as handouts, letters, and flyers for staff, students, or their families; lists of web sites on various topics (suicide, school shootings, signs of depression, the developmental stages of grief in children, and so on); and lists of hotline numbers for national support groups.

While these materials do not fall strictly under the category of media relations, media relations staff may provide assistance in creating these documents, and it is helpful for the PIO to know what materials the school may distribute to the public in an emergency. He or she can then use information from those materials to encourage the press to publish important information. (See the *Crisis Resource Manual* for additional information.)

Identify Possible Locations for a News Conference

Designate a centralized place where news conferences can be held, and arrange for space you could use on short notice in case of an emergency. Sometimes city hall, the library, a senior center, or another public building has a suitable auditorium or meeting room. The room needs to be big enough to accommodate the anticipated number of media and their equipment as well as school officials and media relations personnel. In an emergency or in large cities with several newspapers and multiple television and radio stations, you may need a place that will hold hundreds of people.

Since media operations are largely self-contained, you should not have to worry about the technical end of the news conference. However, having equipment available—especially if your designated news conference room is "wired"—can be a nice amenity for visiting media. Sometimes districts will have portable equipment for such events. Audiovisual packages can be rented from an audiovisual or sound-system business.

Identify Possible Locations for a Crisis Communications Center

Designate two possible locations for a crisis communications center (CCC). The CCC is where spokespersons from all responding agencies can meet, where coordinated decisions and statements can be formulated, where information can be broadcast to the media, and where reporters can call, fax, or e-mail for updated information during a crisis.

If your district is large enough to have several PIOs (one each for individual schools or regions, as well as for the district as a whole), plan to have the district's public information officer work with you in the same room and in full collaboration with the PIOs from other agencies and organizations involved in crisis response. This high level of coordination will help to ensure that all PIOs are aware of the information being given to the media and will minimize the media's ability to surprise a superintendent or others in leadership positions with information released by another agency.

In some cases, the CCC may also be a good location for news conferences. The CCC should be removed from the crisis site and easily accessible to reporters. Be sure to let the reporters know its location as soon as possible—ahead of time, if possible. Also be sure to locate the CCC where there are good support facilities (restrooms or portable toilets, restaurants, hotels, and so on).

Depending on the nature of the crisis, it may be desirable to find a central location outside or near the CCC for a media center, where reporters can work and where their vehicles can be staged. However, finding a separate place is not always worth the effort—media will often have their own mobile equipment and may choose to park as close as possible to the crisis communications center.

Research Phone Lines

Before a crisis, someone from your district should contact your phone company to determine if rapid installation of "trunk-hunting" or rollover lines will be possible. This task is best done by a person responsible for school operations, but the PIO will need to know how calls will be handled in order to inform the public correctly in a crisis.

Trunk-hunting lines work like a switchboard and allow a greater number of incoming calls to the same number: If the number called is busy or unavailable, the call is automatically switched to the next number in what is called a "hunt group." The lead number should not be the number of the school or the district office. Instead, it might be the number of city hall or a new number only used in crises. If the phone company suggests assigning a new number, it may be possible to identify that number ahead of time. If you use an existing number, be sure that the location can be staffed 24 hours a day. Many people will call late at night, anxious and needing comfort and contact more than information. Find out which number your school will use in a crisis, and include it in your sample crisis press releases for ease of reference later.

Trunk-hunting lines need to be installed at either the emergency operations center (the center for general crisis response) or the crisis communications center (the center for the media relations aspect of the crisis), so the person handling this task should check the trunk-hunting viability of all the possible locations that have been identified. Be certain that in an emergency, the phone company could install 10–20 trunk-hunting lines within an hour of the district's request.

Planning for Effective Media Relations

If you do not know them already, find out the numbers assigned to any phone lines in your building used for accessing the Internet or faxing. These lines are often unlisted and may be used to make outside calls in a crisis or as contact numbers for a specific group. Check that your phones will work from the data jacks.

Media Relations Resource Checklist

• • • • • • • • • • • • • • • • • • •

Assemble a packet containing easy-to-read copies of:

- ____ The media relations plan
- ____ Team roles and responsibilities

- ____ An emergency directory
- ____ An organizational chart and directory
- ____ A media directory
- ____ A volunteer staff directory, including phone bank operators and trauma counselors

- ____ Possible locations for a crisis communication center
- ____ Possible locations for a news conference
- ____ Meeting management and facilitation basics

- ____ Media tools checklists (PSA, press release, media advisory, news conference)
- ____ Media tools samples (PSA, press release, media advisory, news conference agenda)
- ____ Media tools templates (electronic)
- ____ A press kit

- ____ Handouts for staff and families of affected students (see pages 101 and 107)
- ____ Web site and hotline resources

- ____ Other forms, flyers, and letter templates that may be released to the public in a crisis
- ____ Guidelines and tips in school-to-parent communications
- ____ Guidelines and tips in school-to-staff communications

Train and Practice

Training for ongoing media relations may be "on the job," for the most part, especially in a small district. If your school has special media relations problems or is in a large metropolitan district, it may be useful to hire media relations experts for some short-term training.

In a crisis, however, media relations training and practice are essential to successful media management. Public information officers, as well as their communications teams, should be thoroughly trained and seasoned in crisis communications. If the PIO or any member of the communications team is a teacher, administrator, or counselor, he or she needs to become more familiar with both media relations and crisis management.

A training curriculum should include topics such as media relations, public speaking, leadership, teamwork, writing, communications issues, media industry trends and practices, and district confidentiality policies. Additionally, it should provide clear information about local emergency response agencies and how they operate in collaboration. The district should commit to a training and team-building budget to support that purpose. Practice and role play *before* a crisis occurs.

Once you have determined who will handle media relations, that person needs to make an effort to develop good working relationships with members of the media. The press liaison or PIO should take the time to meet local reporters and establish a working relationship before a school crisis occurs. There is no single other key that will provide a district with more leverage in a crisis than having established a good working relationship with the media prior to the event.

Likewise, aim to develop good working relationships with responding agency PIOs in advance of a crisis: Meet regularly with local agencies to share plans and find agreement on procedures, protocol, and formats to follow in a crisis.

Making Positive Connections

You can use your new crisis media communications plan as the subject for your first press release or news conference. Use this opportunity to acquire basic information about who to contact in a crisis (and how), to make personal contact with some significant media personnel, and to set a friendly collaborative tone.

Contact each of the stations and newspapers in your area, and ask to speak with either the editor or a reporter who would be likely to cover a crisis. Chat with them informally for a few minutes about the fact that you are organizing press response materials as part of crisis planning for your school. Tell them you expect to send a media advisory soon to call a meeting of those interested in working with you to establish open lines of communication. The benefit to them of your planning efforts is that you will contact them quickly and smoothly on crisis day to be certain that they receive any information. If you need to contact many stations and papers, consider breaking up the list between several communications team members.

Using your template, send out a media alert announcing the meeting. For the actual news conference, write a short press release outlining your desire to do the following:

- Convene interested media representatives to discuss how best to communicate during a crisis.

- Hear media concerns and desires regarding the dissemination of information and the crisis communications plan outlined by your district.

- Build trust toward a time when working together could be mutually beneficial.

- Verify that the school has as much information as possible to meet the media's needs.

After this meeting, issue a press release on a more everyday subject of interest to the media. You might highlight the retirement of a much-loved teacher, for example, or the school's efforts to find community partners for a new after-school program. Then watch the newspaper to see if your story gets coverage.

Do not pester reporters to cover the story; spend your energy writing a great press release instead. If your story gets coverage, write a brief thank-you note to the reporter and to the editor. If your story does not get covered, call one of the more sympathetic reporters you spoke with at the news conference, and ask why. Get feedback so that you can write a more effective press release next time. The next chapter will show how having established media relations and a well-trained staff is essential in a crisis.

Media Relations Planning Checklist

• • • • • • • • • • • • • • • • • •

____ Establish a district-wide media relations policy.

____ Create a written plan for ongoing and crisis media relations.

____ Create media relations goals that are strategic and specific, measurable, attainable, results-oriented, and time-bound.

____ Be sure that goals are consistent with your budget and staffing.

____ Identify and assign key roles and responsibilities.

____ Identify and assemble media relations resources.

____ Inform the press of your media relations policy.

____ Train and practice.

Media Relations for Schools • Copyright © 2007 by Cheri Lovre
Solution Tree • www.solution-tree.com

Chapter 4

Using Media Effectively During a Crisis

Chapter Overview

Sections

- Activate the Crisis Communications Team (page 95)
- Establish the Crisis Communications Center (page 95)
- Install Trunk-Hunting Lines (page 96)
- Disseminate Emergency Information (page 97)
- Establish Content and Boundaries (page 99)
- Inform Stakeholders (page 103)
- Hold a News Conference (page 109)
- Track Media Relations (page 115)
- Debrief Team and Staff (page 115)
- Nourish Self and Staff (page 116)

Handouts and Checklists

- How to Handle Media Calls (page 101)
- How to Handle the News Media (page 107)
- Crisis Media Relations Checklist (page 118)

IN A CRISIS

> This guide is only intended to cover media relations in a crisis; there are many other aspects to crisis management. Please consult the *Crisis Resource Manual,* the *Catastrophic Events Resource Manual,* and *The Safe Room* for more information.

Act quickly in a crisis. Call reporters you know as soon as you can if your crisis has any of the following characteristics:

- The event causes parents to panic or lose their trust in the school.

- Parents want to pick up their children before the end of the school day.

- The media will probably report on what happened.

- Traffic lanes must be open for emergency vehicles.

Be assertive with the media. The media liaison or public information officer should take control of the situation with the media as much as possible and convince them to present information from the school's perspective:

- Call them before they call you.

- Request reporters with whom you already have a working relationship.

- Suggest a time and neutral place where you can meet with them.

- Tell them you will have an official statement ready for them at that time.

- Only release information from that off-site location; keep the media away from the crisis site.

- Request that they help you announce vital information to the community.

Asking reporters to broadcast information that will help your district's families or assist emergency responders in their efforts can make a tremendous difference in how well your community responds to the crisis.

Activate the Crisis Communications Team

Consult your crisis plan, and contact every member of the crisis communications team, including backup staff and auxiliary members such as parent volunteers. Tell staff where to meet (or to stay on "standby") and what to bring. Remind them of your district's confidentiality guidelines. Decide who will be the initial contact for media queries. Make sure the media compiler knows to start doing his or her job.

Establish the Crisis Communications Center

Establish the location where PIOs and agency representatives will be based. Set up desks, phones, fax machines, and computers; send the go-fer out for healthy snacks and drinks; contact the press to let them know the crisis communications center (CCC) is open and how to contact it; contact clerical staff at the schools to let them know where to refer the press.

Always have at least one representative from the school at the crisis communications center. Any time the lead PIO is absent during operating hours, someone equally prepared must be available as a substitute. Emergencies may require the attention of the general crisis response team (which includes communications personnel) on a round-the-clock schedule during the first few days.

Depending on the scale of the media's response, you may also want to establish a separate media center for reporters to work out of (with desks, fax machines, phones, and so on). They may or may not use it, given how independently media rigs operate. Release information there regularly to keep them satisfied and (as much as possible) stationary. Otherwise, create parking spaces for their vehicles in proximity to the CCC or where news conferences will occur.

Then, take the following steps:

- Install trunk-hunting lines.

- Disseminate emergency information.

- Establish content and boundaries.

- Inform stakeholders.

- Hold a news conference.

- Track media relations.

- Debrief team and staff.

- Nourish self and staff.

Install Trunk-Hunting Lines

Someone from the district crisis response team should contact the phone company to install trunk-hunting phone lines; ideally, your school or district crisis response plan will have already designated a person for that task. He or she will ask for

10–20 trunk-hunting phone lines (installed in your emergency operations center or crisis communications center). Trunk-hunting lines should take about an hour to set up.

Once installed, trunk-hunting lines can be staffed by city or county employees and school district clerical or other staff. This can be set up so that one person does "triage" by answering and redirecting calls: "This is the emergency line. What is the nature of your call?" There will mostly be three kinds of calls: frantic family members looking for their loved ones, counselors offering assistance for victims, and reporters wanting the story. The person doing triage should simply transfer calls to the person or people handling each specific type of request.

The media relations team should not be responsible for setting up phone lines, but you will need to know what phone number to release to the press and public. As soon as you know the number that will access the trunk-hunting lines, fax or e-mail all press contacts, and ask them to begin giving out that number as the one number to call for all concerns related to the crisis. Keep school phone lines available for your own use; you can use Internet access and fax lines to create extra lines for outgoing calls.

Disseminate Emergency Information

Getting the press to air emergency information is the most crucial media relations issue, especially early on, when confusion reigns. It is a virtual certainty that normal telephone switches, including 911, will become inundated in the first hours of a crisis. *If the media broadcasts phone numbers to call and/or locations where the public can get their questions answered and needs met, the calls that are jamming the phone lines will drop off quickly.* For this reason, it is very important to alert the broadcast media to where the public can call for information, as well as any other pertinent data, such as where students from an affected school have been taken, how parents can find and reunite with their children, and when and where meetings will be held.

When parents and other concerned citizens call for specific information, they will often try to call the school, the district, or city offices. Think of the places people might likely be calling for information when they cannot get through to the schools. Add those organizations to the database of other numbers and e-mail addresses that should receive updates. Mental health clinics, hospitals, the local Red Cross, anything in the yellow pages under "crisis," nearby school districts, and the mayor's office are some examples of those who may be inundated with calls from panicking parents and concerned community members. They are often willing to answer questions when calls come in, as long as they have the basic information, and they will appreciate knowing the number parents can call for additional details.

The faster you do these things, the quicker the community will begin to calm down, tune in to TV or radio for their news, and allow the phone system to become operational again. Send an initial press release to do the following:

- Acknowledge that the event has occurred.

- State what measures the school will have in place.

- Give the date, time, and location of the news conference, if one is needed.

- Alert the media that they will not be allowed on campus.

- Advise the media of their primary contact for information.

Establish Content and Boundaries

All communications to media should emanate from the crisis communications team and be specifically cleared by the lead public information officer. Public information distributed to the media about a crisis should always be authorized beforehand by the administrator overseeing the crisis (or that person's designee). This cuts down on rumors and becomes increasingly important as the crisis unfolds and numerous response agencies provide their own PIO or communications staff to help out. In addition, consider contacting your school or district attorney to make sure you avoid any statements that might trigger litigation later. Be sure to:

- Coordinate the content of all statements.

- Control the content of all statements.

- Discourage "scoop" mentality.

All information should focus on reiterating facts and updating information in a timely fashion. Do not try to follow up or respond to every rumor. Establish yourself as the credible source for factual information, and the rumors will fade.

Coordinate Content

Work closely with the crisis communications team and those present at the crisis communications center. Share information via e-mail or fax with all emergency personnel and with those PIOs not present to assure that everyone has access to and is releasing consistent information. Collaborative work with the PIOs from other agencies can be very gratifying; great efficiency can come from cooperation. Whenever possible, strive for *joint* news releases from a single source, preferably the crisis communications center. However, if law enforcement releases separate news releases, ask if the crisis communications team can receive those news releases in advance of issuing their own; otherwise, PIOs are unable to confirm some details the media may have obtained from law enforcement and thus may appear less credible.

If not all of the PIOs involved are working collaboratively out of a single CCC—hospitals, for instance, may want to keep theirs in-house—it is still most effective to have them or their representatives participate at any formal news conferences. Some information, such as patient condition, is subject to privacy laws; only the hospital should answer questions on patneit condition. Be sure that you are also "on the list" to receive ongoing updates about funeral locations, dates, and times; check in with area mortuaries and funeral homes.

Control Content

Provide people staffing the phones with clear guidelines on what to say and how to say it: Create a written script, if necessary. Most calls from the media will want to know the same basic things. Phone workers should be ready to add reporters to the master list for press releases and updates, and they should reassure reporters that the school is sending out informational faxes and e-mails often. Remind phone staff that they have every right to ask callers to hang up to free the line for more crucial calls; they do not have to offer anything more than the opportunity to get on the contact list, at least until the situation at the school stabilizes.

How to Handle Media Calls

A Handout for Staff

1. Never be rude. Reporters may insult your status, your intelligence, or your feelings, but do not let them provoke a response. Use professionalism to fight back.

2. Screen the call: Ask who is calling, what organization they represent, and how to contact them with more information.

3. Direct questions to the appropriate person, and defer any that you are not authorized to answer:

    "_____ is the best person to answer that. I can transfer your call, or I can take your phone number and [he or she] will call you back."

    "I'll make sure that someone returns your call with the answers to these questions."

    "I'll find out the answer to that question and will call you as soon as I know."

4. Remember that even if you tell the caller you will call him or her back personally, it may be best to refer the question to the PIO or media contact and have that person make the return call.

5. If a conversation goes too far, end it politely: "I'm sorry, but I must reserve this line for emergency calls."

In addition, bar media access to events that may have unpredictable conversations or outbursts. If you provide meetings or gatherings for students or families, for example, carefully consider whether the media should be allowed to attend. On one hand, inviting the media shows that the school is working diligently to meet the needs of the community for information and reassurance. Reporters may also be able to base positive, helpful stories on any handouts you create to inform or support students and parents.

On the other hand, parents benefit from having time with other parents, and a closed meeting allows them to voice their fears and concerns in privacy. Media presence usually compromises the value of discussion; some parents may grandstand or publicize their anger in exaggerated ways. As a compromise, you can always fax or e-mail pertinent handouts to your media contacts, or invite them to an initial portion of the meeting when school administrators and others will be setting the tone and distributing information.

You do not have to announce these private meetings to reporters, but be prepared to answer their questions about the meetings. For example, they may ask you, on camera, why the media was excluded. Be prepared to respond in a way that emphasizes why a closed meeting helped the school community:

> "Our students have been remarkably respectful and supportive of each other while we've been under media scrutiny. We want to give them some time together in the privacy they deserve."

Having a private gathering (such as a funeral) in a public place (such as the school gym) can make it more difficult to limit access to the media. If you know your facility will be used for a funeral, work with your attorney as soon as possible to outline ways to limit media access. One option is to create a media pool (for more information, see page 109).

Discourage "Scoop" Mentality

Level the playing field by refusing to grant exclusive interviews. If all reporters have the same access to the same information, their broadcasts will be more factual, and turf wars can be reduced. It may be tempting to give some priority to local media with whom you have established relationships, since they live in your community and might be more likely to respect boundaries and work cooperatively. However, playing favorites can backfire. If possible, treat local and national media equally.

Inform Stakeholders

By this time in a crisis, you will have contacted emergency services, your school administration, and your school attorney to coordinate and authorize content. Other parties, both on- and offsite, will also need information. These include school board members, elected officials, staff, students, and parents.

School Board Members and Elected Officials

In a crisis, elected officials (school board members, the PTA president, and so on) are likely to show up at the school or the CCC. If you do not brief them, they may give interviews inconsistent with the messages you are trying to disseminate through news organizations. If dozens of reporters or reporting teams respond, each will be looking for numerous interviews with anyone they can find, anyone willing to speak who has some association with the crisis. So let elected officials be involved. Call them before they call you or arrive on the scene. Give them work doing interviews, and help them with talking points. Get them ready, and then debrief them to build their confidence.

Remember, they were not elected to do this particular job. Be generous with your help and gracious with your praise.

Staff and Students

All students and staff members should be reminded that they are not obligated to talk with a reporter, especially during a crisis. Keep in mind, however, that you cannot prohibit students from speaking with the media (that would violate their Free Speech rights), and that these guidelines do not necessarily apply during athletic games and other normal public events.

Share the following with every student and staff member in an announcement made at staff meetings and classes:

> You are not obligated to talk to a member of the news media in a crisis. In fact, the school requests that you do not. Comments can be taken out of context, and the resulting inaccurate stories are worse than no story at all. If a reporter approaches you, we request that you refer them to _____, who is our contact person for the news media. You might do that by saying, "Many people are asking similar

questions. _____ is the best person to talk to about that."

The school administration will work with the media to give them an accurate and positive picture of what is happening at the school. If you would like to share a message, please speak with _____. If you see reporters, people with cameras, or others who may be with the media on school grounds, please notify _____.

We all have the right to grieve in privacy and with dignity. Our task as a school is to commemorate _____'s life and give meaning to *[his or her]* death for us and for our school community. The school will support this above all other issues at this time.

To further shield students from confrontations with the media, station several support people—trained volunteers, Red Cross volunteers, or parents—at any memorial spots that may be spontaneously arising as the focal point for community grief, flowers, cards, candles, and so on, where students can be suddenly overcome by the magnitude of the event. Reporters often violate the sanctity of that space to get a story.

Parents

Your initial press release should already have reminded the press to direct parents to the trunk-hunting lines for phone calls and to tell them where to pick up their children and which streets to avoid for emergency vehicles. You can also ask the media to announce parent and community meetings; if you do not want the media to attend those meetings, look for other ways to notify the community.

Modify your school's web site to include updated information, the number to call for information or help, crisis hotlines, and any other information parents might need. If news of affected students or staff is part of the information you release, be sure to share press release and news conference materials with the families of those affected people before airing them with the media.

It can be very supportive to families of victims if the PIO is willing to communicate with media on the family's behalf. Most people have no idea what obligation they have, if any, to respond to news media. An experienced PIO should assist wherever possible. The crisis communications team can run interference for the families and shield them from the media, they can coordinate interview opportunities with families who are willing, or they can include families as speakers at the press conference and assist them with creating statements. You might also release the "How to Handle the News Media" handout (page 107) to help affected families understand their own rights with regard to the media.

How to Handle the News Media

• •

A Handout for Families

Reporters want a story, and they can be intrusive in their pursuit of that story. There are risks in talking to reporters: They may report on what you say in a way you did not intend, they may put their own spin on the story, or they may simply interfere with your grieving process.

If you do work with the media, you can take steps to increase the likelihood that they will report the story in a sensitive and accurate way. First, protect your children from the media. It is rarely helpful for children in grief to talk with the press. Second, meet with reporters on your own terms. Ask yourself:

Will I speak with reporters? You are not obligated to speak with any reporter. Your family has the right to grieve in privacy, with dignity.

If so, where and when will I speak with them? Reporters do not have the right to be on private property, even if that is the scene of the tragedy, but they often follow investigators around. You have the right to tell them to leave. If your tragedy involves court hearings or trials, be prepared for media presence there, too.

You can choose when and where you will interact with the media. You can ask school officials to include you as part of their news conference; there you would be surrounded by familiar faces from the school, and your statement would not be the whole focus. Your church, synagogue, or city hall may also be willing to offer space.

Who will I speak to? If you know and trust someone in the media, you can grant an interview to that person alone. You are not obligated to talk to other reporters.

What information will I share, and in what form? How will I respond to questions about how I feel or whether justice was done? What kinds of responses will maintain my dignity in public? Simply speaking honestly with a reporter does not guarantee that your views will be accurately reported. As an alternative to an interview, you can provide a written statement, which can give you more control over content. You even may want to write your own guest opinion or letter to the editor if there are points about the incident that you want the news media to cover.

If you speak with a reporter, you have the right to ask how the story will be presented, which quotes of yours will be used, or any other questions. You can ask reporters to cover your side of the story completely, rather than focusing on dramatic parts of the story that may give more attention to the crime or the perpetrator than to victims. You cannot control what is reported, but you can control what you share, and you can ask how it will be used.

How will I handle photography? If you are interviewed, you have the right to decide whether photographs will be taken. If reporters have pictures of the tragedy that are hurtful to your family, you can ask that they not be used. You may not have legal authority to prevent them from using the photos, but you may find sympathetic reporters. If the death was in your family, it may be helpful to provide the media with a photograph of the deceased that you would like them to use.

Are there others who can help me? You can choose someone you trust to represent you to the media. Your county or state victim's assistance department may be able to help you handle the media and any legal or other issues. If a student is injured or killed in a crime-related incident, the local victim assistance program usually assigns a victim advocate to the family to help family members cope with the legal system. Contact your district attorney's office for a referral.

Finally, if you are rudely or inappropriately treated by a reporter, you can file a complaint with the newspaper editor, TV or radio producer, or the reporter's supervisor. If a story contains inaccurate information, you can request a prompt correction.

Hold a News Conference

If national media is involved, try to arrange news conferences early in the day, so that reporters can file their stories on time, despite any time zone differences. If the need warrants it, consider using a media pool. In a media pool, only one media representative or small group of representatives represents each sector of news media (wire services, TV, radio, print, photographers, and so on). That person or small group then attends news conferences, or "briefings," and shares the information with all others in their respective sector. You may find a trusted local reporter to volunteer to organize the pool with you, or you may wish to let the media representatives assembled make that choice as a group—that will remove some potential criticism of the administrator or PIO for making a unilateral decision. Media pools are particularly helpful for coverage of funerals, vigils, or other events in which a large media presence will significantly detract from the ambiance, goal, or function of the gathering.

Do not rush into a news conference. Reporters are willing to wait, and you do not want to defeat the purpose by being disorganized. Give yourself time to complete the following tasks:

- Establish the location.

- Choose speakers.

- Send a media advisory.

- Establish content.

- Direct the conference.

- Follow up.

Establish the Location

Check your crisis media plan for possible locations away from the school, then schedule your conference, reserve needed equipment and furnishings, and assign staff to run the conference. For more information on the furnishings, physical set up of the room, and materials you might need, see page 48.

Choose Speakers

Whenever conducting a news conference, get as many PIOs and other spokespersons together as possible ahead of time. To minimize surprises and duplication, ask each to share what his or her comments will be. When other agency representatives are not able to be at the news conference, get their input ahead of time. E-mail is a great way to coordinate and distribute news updates. Having joint news conferences and sharing information in this fashion trains media and the public alike to look to the emergency response team and the crisis communications center staff as reliable sources for authoritative information. It suggests that all personnel are working together on the same goals. It sends the message, "We know what we're doing, and we are in agreement about what is being said."

Reporters often want to ask students questions. Although in general it is recommended that you inservice students with the request that they not speak with reporters who approach them, it can be very helpful to have students speak on behalf of the student body—under controlled circumstances and with parental permission. If you decide to do so and can find two or three mature students who are willing to speak, follow these guidelines:

Using Media Effectively During a Crisis

- Make sure students know they are not obligated, and obtain parental permission.

- Include parents at every step of the process to ensure that they understand what will happen.

- Ask reporters what they hope to get from students and what kinds of questions they are likely to ask.

- Help students organize their thoughts into a written statement to read aloud. Feel free to suggest some talking points that you think are fair representations of the reflections of the general student population.

- Make sure the administration has a chance to review and approve everything the students will say, and ensure that students know not to ad lib.

- Tell reporters that someone will signal to students whether they can answer questions and that the conference will be interrupted if a question is inappropriate or involves confidential or sensitive topics.

- Let students know that a school representative will either nod an "okay" to answer each question or will step in to respond.

- Tell students that even if they get the nod to answer, they can still turn the question over to an adult.

- Review with students and reporters any areas that you do not want them to cover, just in case.

- Give students honest answers they can give when asked difficult questions ("I can't speak about whether other students were involved. The police are investigating; that would be a question for them").

Send a Media Advisory

If you have not done so already, notify the media when and where the press conference will be and who will be present, using a formal media advisory or, if you need to consolidate information to save time, a press release. Consult your crisis media plan for samples and guidelines. Obtain administrative approval for the event. If you are having trouble keeping reporters off school grounds (often the media will set up their base of operations at the school memorial wall site), consider distributing the announcement only to press vehicles located offsite, to send the message that onsite media representatives will be missing important notifications and opportunities to meet with school administrators and emergency response representatives.

Establish Content

Following your crisis plan guidelines and coordinating with other spokespersons, create a statement, and submit it to your administration for approval.

Usually, initial information about a tragedy or crisis will be incomplete or inaccurate. Accordingly, it is wise to qualify the source or accuracy of remarks made at a news conference:

- "Our initial information from the police department indicates . . ."

- "The investigators say it appears likely . . ."

- "Information from the police indicates we may have four injured students . . ."

Think through a list of likely questions you will receive at the news conference. *Never say, "No comment."* Instead, use responses like:

- "We're waiting to see the police report before we can comment."

- "That question really lies in the domain of the investigation. I'd rather you get a comment from the police department [or district attorney's office] on that."

- "In the interest of maintaining the privacy and integrity of the family, the school is not taking any position on that."

Remember, do not waste time trying to squelch rumors—focus on publishing facts and having updates come out in a timely fashion. If a rumored fact needs verification, reporters will ask you. When faxing or releasing information to media, establish a pattern that ensures that each of several topic areas will be consistently covered. Include information about such things as the investigation; patient condition; measures the school, city, and county are putting into place; location of children (if they have been evacuated); and when you expect to have the next news conference. Be certain that the media compiler and/or record-keeper is archiving all lists, notes, agendas, and press releases generated during this time.

Direct the Conference

Firmly establish ground rules at the first news conference. By your presence and attitude, convey that you are in charge and that this is *your* turf. If you want reporters to raise their hands to be recognized, ask them to do so. Maintaining order in the proceedings will prevent a "stampede" mentality. Review the News Conference Checklist on page 55, if necessary.

You will also be a facilitator for other spokespersons, making sure that they and their messages are heard. The bottom line is that the media must go where you lead to get information. If there are important facts to get out, take charge and get them out—but be fair.

Answering Tough Media Questions

- Do not blame anyone for anything.

- Do not speak "off the record."

- Do not ad-lib.

- Do not speculate.

- Never say, "No comment."

- Emphasize the positive and what you know for certain.

- Do not repeat negative or misleading words that a reporter has used in a question.

- Do not argue with reporters.

- Tell the truth.

- Speak from personal experience.

- Be positive.

- Feel free to say, "I don't know."

- Correct inaccuracies.

- If you have limits, identify them.

(Adapted from Woodland, 2003)

Follow Up

News conferences should be videotaped, or at least audio taped, and then archived by the media compiler for possible future use. Once the conference is over, gather the speakers for a debriefing. What questions came up? What needs to be clarified? Who will follow up to see that reporters get what they need? When will the next news conference or briefing occur?

Track Media Relations

Copies of all faxes and information sent out should be filed as well, along with information as it appears in the paper. Compare your press releases with published or aired coverage to be sure that your message is getting through. Correct any inaccuracies. Update your media directory to reflect new contacts.

Debrief Team and Staff

All team and staff members should be reminded of the importance of confidentiality at every gathering of staff following a crisis, particularly at the first gathering.

All team and staff members working on communications and media relations also need to be debriefed for trauma prevention at the end of every day, by someone skilled in trauma intervention. This means, for instance, that if someone works until two in the afternoon and then moves on to some other responsibility, that person needs a debriefing before he or she leaves the building. Consult your crisis plan for a list of trauma counselors, and arrange for someone to work onsite.

Nourish Self and Staff

Take breaks when you can. This work is exhausting and will continue to be so for some time. Remember to eat. Stock plenty of nutritious snacks and fluids—do not try to get by on pizza and coffee. Remember, the crisis communications center may be operating on a round-the-clock basis for 3 or 4 days, but you and your staff may still be putting in very long days beyond that, as new information breaks.

A Collaborative Success Story

The aftermath of the shooting at Thurston High School in Springfield, Oregon, revealed what a critical difference an effective media relations plan can make in the midst of tragedy. On the morning of the shooting, the district PIO was at city hall with the city PIO and an emergency services PIO by 10:00 am. The group of collaborating PIOs continued to grow as more agencies and organizations became involved. The Red Cross, the two hospitals, the county mental health clinic, and many others joined in the combined effort. Even the representatives for the investigating police and the district attorney joined together.

This process provided many benefits: No administrator or director of any agency was ever ambushed by media asking about information released by another agency. All heads of agencies spoke with one voice at a single press conference, flawlessly coordinated and facilitated by the city's PIO.

The final trauma debriefings held for crisis response staff were attended by a total of 13 public information officers who had represented their agencies in this collaborative effort. At times, representatives from clergy and business clubs were involved as well.

All of this was facilitated more easily because the school and the city had already established good working relationships with local media. The frenzy that comes with the arrival of national and international news groups could never have been handled with such grace, had it not been for the local effort to collaborate.

Although it can never be known for certain, this collaboration of media liaisons may be why neither the district nor any district administrators or staff were named in any litigation. This may be the only school shooting with mass casualties that generated no lawsuits toward anyone other than the estate of the perpetrator's family.

Crisis Media Relations Checklist

Phase 1: Immediate Response

_____ Meet with principal and other crisis response team members.

_____ Brief team on district media policy; enact policy as part of first response.

_____ Meet with crisis communications team, and delegate roles and tasks.

_____ Activate the crisis communications center (away from the crisis location).

_____ Work with crisis response team on coordination of phone resources and installation of trunk-hunting lines.

_____ Confer with PIOs from other responding agencies to coordinate the content of news releases and news conferences.

_____ Exchange press release information via e-mail or fax with PIOs unable to be at the CCC.

_____ Fax or e-mail information to all agencies and organizations that may be receiving calls from parents who cannot get through to schools. Give them the basic facts and the trunk-hunting phone number parents can call for more information.

_____ Fax or e-mail media organizations with your first crisis press release. Include crisis news, news conference schedule, pertinent phone numbers, spokespersons available for interviews, and web site addresses with press kits or other basic school information (such as school name, school size, principal's name, grade levels, and so on). You might also mention whether a crisis plan is in effect and whether the school has had practice drills.

In the news release, ask the media to emphasize the following to the public:

- The number to call for information regarding the emergency

- Where parents can reunite with their children

- What streets to avoid so that emergency vehicles have clear access

____ Schedule a news conference at a neutral site.

____ Call elected officials to let them know how they can be involved. Give a briefing and clear guidance on what can and cannot be stated publicly.

____ Activate a designated web site with updated information and phone numbers.

Phase 2: Secondary Tasks

____ Work with the crisis response team to develop communications (handouts, phone scripts, and meeting agendas and materials) for staff, families, and parents.

____ Return as many deferred calls as possible.

____ Hold the first news conference (being mindful of time-zone differences).

____ Clear any public statements with school administration and the crisis response team. Make sure statements are coordinated with other PIOs to avoid giving conflicting information.

____ Continue faxing and e-mailing updates to the press regularly.

____ If appropriate, establish a media center for reporters.

____ Be a resource at staff meetings, especially in terms of generating and disseminating information.

Phase 3: Follow Up

_____ Work with the crisis response team to prepare materials for daily debriefings.

_____ Handle communications for parents, staff, school board, and community (aside from news conferences) as needed. For example, write, edit, or review letters and flyers about the school's reopening and new safety efforts.

_____ Make sure the media compiler is doing a proper job of acquiring and archiving information; after the crisis has subsided, collect and archive all notes, clippings, videos, and so on made during the crisis.

Media Relations for Schools • Copyright © 2007 by Cheri Lovre
Solution Tree • www.solution-tree.com

The Last Word: A Glossary

Crisis communications center: The working location for the crisis communications team. This may be shared space with the emergency operations center or a separate space.

Crisis communications team: The team responding specifically to the media relations and communications of the school community in the aftermath of crisis or tragedy. This team may be composed only of school personnel, but most effectively, it will be a collaborative effort between the public information officers for all responding agencies: the police, the fire department, the mayor's office, the hospital, the Red Cross, FEMA, and a variety of other possible agencies.

Crisis response team: The team responding to the overall needs of the school community in the aftermath of crisis or tragedy. Ideally, this team has trained together before the crisis. Crisis Management Insitute materials refer to these as "Flight Teams" as they "fly in" at a moment's notice to meet the needs of another building in crisis.

Emergency operations center (EOC): The national emergency management system's term for the location of operations for the collaborative emergency response team. The EOC may be housed in city hall or at a site determined by the person in charge of declaring a state of emergency (the incident commander).

Emergency response team: One or more designees who work with the incident commander at the emergency operations center. In the best case, these lead people work together to streamline the coordination of multiagency incident-response efforts. This might include the police, fire department, SWAT team, emergency services related to natural disasters, or other agencies that are mobilized based on the needs of the event.

Federal Emergency Management Agency (FEMA): FEMA's mission is to lead the effort to prepare the nation for all hazards and effectively manage federal response and recovery efforts following any national incident.

Incident Command System (ICS): The Incident Command System is a standardized on-scene incident management system developed by FEMA to organize facilities, equipment, personnel, procedures, and communications. ICS has been incorporated into the national incident management system (NIMS).

Incident commander: The national emergency management system's term for the chief or commander of the department in charge of the response (usually a local official). All agencies providing mutual aid operate under the incident commander.

Media advisory: A notice announcing an upcoming press conference (sometimes called a media alert).

Media pool: A media pool allows one media representative or a small group of representatives to represent each sector of news media (wire services, TV, radio, print, photographers, and so on). Representatives attend news conferences or "briefings" and share the information with all others in their respective sector through a live feed or other agreed-upon method.

Memorial wall: The site where community members spontaneously memorialize victims by leaving letters, flowers, candles, teddy bears, crosses, and other tokens of sympathy. If the school is surrounded by a fence, the memorial wall is often some portion of the fence.

Mutual aid: The term used by emergency services for the assistance of nearby communities when an event overwhelms one jurisdiction's ability to respond.

National incident management system (NIMS): The Federal Emergency Management Agency (FEMA) designed the national incident management system (NIMS) to be certain that duplication is avoided, that equipment interfaces, and that everyone is clear about who is in charge. NIMS clarifies who has the responsibility and authority to make various kinds of decisions at various levels. It is a command system similar to a military command, clarifying how information and actions move through "the ranks" of the many agencies and organizations that might respond to any given crisis. It ensures that when an agency arrives at a disaster site, its commander knows who can answer questions and give permission for action. Different kinds of crises may result in different organizations having the position of highest authority. During a pandemic, for example, the health department would have authority over the police and fire departments in deciding when to quarantine a city or region.

News conference: An opportunity for many media representatives to receive information at once (sometimes called a press conference). A news conference usually includes a short statement and a question-and-answer period.

Press release: A one- or two-page document sent to media representatives to encourage coverage of a particular story (sometimes called a media or news release). A press release is written in third person and follows strict formatting rules.

Public information officer: The person within an organization (a school or district, a hospital, or a crisis response agency) who has special training to interact with media and the public and has been designated to serve as the leader for the communications team.

Public service announcement (PSA): An announcement broadcast for free on radio or television to provide the public with information that holds public value.

Trunk-hunting phone lines: Special phone lines installed in a crisis to allow calls to one central number to roll over to the next available line in a list, thus increasing the number of incoming calls to a single number that can be answered.

References and Resources

Czarnecki, A. (2005). Going to the people: Ten public speaking tips. Toronto, Ontario, Canada: Al Czarnecki Communications. Available at www.topstory.ca/speaking.html (accessed November 1, 2005).

Hallahan, K. (1996). A publicity primer. Fort Collins, CO: Author. Available at lamar.colostate.edu/~hallahan/hpubty.htm (accessed November 1, 2005).

International Competition Network. 2005. News conference tips. Available at www.internationalcompetitionnetwork.org/news_conference.html (accessed November 1, 2005).

Miller, A. (2005). PR writing examples. Chicago: Author. Available at work.colum.edu/~amiller/altonmiller (accessed November 1, 2005).

O'Neill, J., & Conzemius, A. (2006). *The power of SMART goals: Using goals to improve student learning.* Bloomington, IN: Solution Tree (formerly National Educational Service).

Ryan, C. (1991). *Prime time activism.* Boston: South End Press.

Schiller, E. (2004). PR notes. Toronto, Ontario, Canada: Schiller & Associates. Available at www.edshiller.com/notesindex.asp (accessed November 1, 2005).

Schindler, E. (2004). The care and feeding of the press. Available at www.netpress.org/careandfeeding.html (accessed November 1, 2005).

Wilcox, D. L., Ault, P. H., and W. K. Agee. (1992). *Public relations: Strategies and tactics* (3rd ed.). New York: HarperCollins.

Woodland, B. (2003). *The media relations survival guide.* Mississauaga, Ontario, Canada: Author.

Make the Most of Your
Professional Development Investment

Let Solution Tree (formerly National Educational Service) schedule time for you and your staff with leading practitioners in the areas of:

- **Professional Learning Communities** with Richard DuFour, Robert Eaker, Rebecca DuFour, and associates
- **Effective Schools** with associates of Larry Lezotte
- **Assessment *for* Learning** with Rick Stiggins and associates
- **Classroom Management** with Lee Canter and associates
- **Crisis Management and Response** with Cheri Lovre
- **Discipline With Dignity** with Richard Curwin and Allen Mendler
- **PASSport to Success** (parental involvement) with Vickie Burt
- **Peacemakers** (violence prevention) with Jeremy Shapiro

Additional presentations are available in the following areas:

- At-Risk Youth Issues
- Bullying Prevention/Teasing and Harassment
- Team Building and Collaborative Teams
- Data Collection and Analysis
- Embracing Diversity
- Literacy Development
- Motivating Techniques for Staff and Students

Solution Tree

304 W. Kirkwood Avenue
Bloomington, IN 47404-5131
(812) 336-7700
(800) 733-6786 (toll-free number)
FAX (812) 336-7790
e-mail: info@solution-tree.com
www.solution-tree.com

NEED MORE COPIES OR ADDITIONAL RESOURCES ON THIS TOPIC?

Need more copies of this book? Want your own copy? Need additional resources on this topic? If so, you can order additional materials by using this form or by calling us toll free at (800) 733-6786 or (812) 336-7700. Or you can order by FAX at (812) 336-7790 or visit our web site at www.solution-tree.com.

Title	Price*	Quantity	Total
Media Relations for Schools (includes CD)	$17.95		
Building Successful Partnerships	18.95		
EdMarketing	24.95		
Grant Writing for Educators	9.95		
The Handbook for SMART School Teams (includes CD-Rom)	54.95		
Learning by Doing (includes CD-Rom)	27.95		
Passion and Persistence (DVD or VHS)	24.95		
Passion and Persistence (screen saver)	9.95		
The Power of SMART Goals	24.95		
The Safe Room (includes CD)	17.95		
		SUBTOTAL	
		SHIPPING	
Continental U.S.: Please add 6% of order total. Outside continental U.S.: Please add 8% of order total.			
		HANDLING	
Continental U.S.: Please add $4. Outside continental U.S.: Please add $6.			
		TOTAL (U.S. funds)	

*Price subject to change without notice.

❏ Check enclosed   ❏ Purchase order enclosed
❏ Money order   ❏ VISA, MasterCard, Discover, or American Express (circle one)

Credit Card No._____ Exp. Date_____
Cardholder Signature _____

SHIP TO:

First Name_____ Last Name_____
Position _____
Institution Name_____
Address_____
City_____ State_____ ZIP_____
Phone_____ FAX_____
E-mail _____

Solution Tree (formerly National Educational Service)
304 W. Kirkwood Avenue
Bloomington, IN 47404-5131
(812) 336-7700 • (800) 733-6786 (toll-free)
FAX (812) 336-7790
e-mail: orders@solution-tree.com
www.solution-tree.com